MW01626981

Between Two Spaces:

Reflections on the Spiritual in Art

Halide Salam

Pocahontas Press, Inc. Blacksburg, Virginia

Between Two Spaces: Reflections on the Spiritual in Art, by Halide Salam

Book design by Suzanne Day
Cover design and photography by Leemar Thorpe

First printing 2008

Published by Pocahontas Press, Inc., Blacksburg, Virginia
800-446-0467 • pocahontaspress.com
Printed by Taylor Specialty Books, Dallas, Texas

ISBN: 0-926487-37-X
978-0926487-37-6

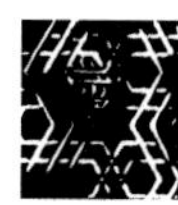

For Ammi: Begum Fatema Reza Salam

Prologue

I have come to recognize that it is from complete understanding of one's chosen disciplines and personal beliefs that one gains empowering knowledge. The power in these bodies of knowledge may transfer to us, if practiced rightly, with sincerity and without prejudice. I have come to trust The Greater Intelligence, One that has set things in motion, in accordance to precise laws, for nothing that has been created can be truly in harmony with itself if it does not comply with the sacred order or *tariqa*—Way—within which all things are to live and move.

So I start this conversation with Praise to the Always-Living, the Self-Subsistent, Existing before everything that existed, exists and will exist, the All-Mighty Compassionate Heart that cradles all that is set and will be set in motion. I start this conversation acknowledging my limitations in grasping the intelligence around me, and aware of my own shortcomings in trying to explain the knowledge that remains unnamed in and outside my senses. I start this conversation subdued, knowing more than what I knew then, but knowing less about now and the future, heartened with the understanding that true wisdom comes only when the heart sieves the knowledge as it passes through the processes of the intellect; and that what we call wisdom is *barakka,* living in the Grace of the Creator.

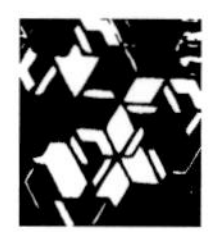

"It is from understanding that power comes; and the power in the ceremony (of the ghost dance) was in understanding what it meant; for nothing can live well except in a manner that is suited to the way the sacred Power of the World lives and moves."

— Black Elk Speaks

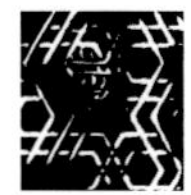

Mirror Mirror
People keep asking me where I come from
says my son.
Trouble is I'm american on the inside
and oriental in the outside
No Doug
Turn that outside in
THIS is what America looks like

— Mitsuye Yamada
Camp Notes and Other Poems

"Every path I take is edged with thorns. On the one hand, I play into the Savior's hands by concentrating on authenticity, for my attention is numbed by it and diverted from other, important issues; on the other hand, I do feel a necessity to return to my so-called roots, since they are the fount of my strength, the guiding arrow to which I constantly refer before heading for a new direction."

—Trinh T. Minh-ha, *Woman Native Other*

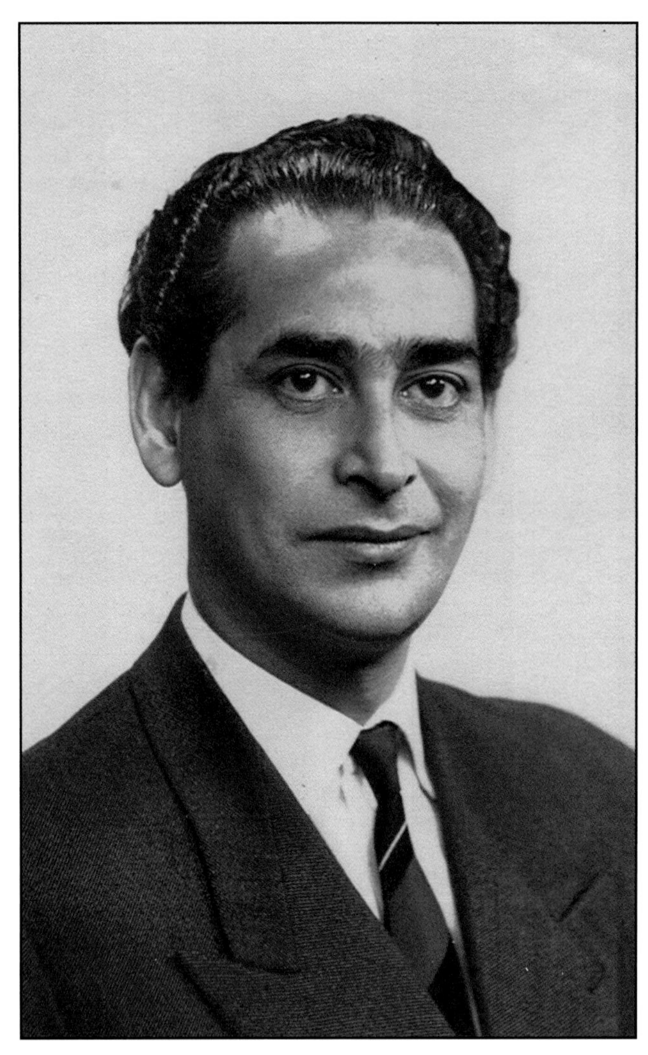

The Ancestral Passage

Father Moon

There is nothing really extraordinary in my life that sets me apart from anyone else. Providence has played a major role in shaping my biological make-up and in prompting actions for which I have no justification. Some may say that my actions are steered by the genes of my ancestors; others insist that it is the prodding of destiny. I like to believe that there are three players in each person's life: their ancestors, destiny, and free will.

I was born to a middle-class Muslim family, the second child among three brothers. My father, Badi usSalam, was the son of Khan Bahadur Abd usSalam of Calcutta, India. The title Khan Bahadur was given to my paternal grandfather by the British, not because he had served as the Personal Secretary of the then Governor General of India, Lord Curzon, but because as the Chief Justice for the Bengal Presidency,[1] he had served India and her people well and was consequently awarded the Earldom of the area known in Calcutta as Central Park.

All Muslim children of the Indian sub-continent refer to their fathers as *Abba* or *Abbo* and their father's father as *Dada,* in order to distinguish them from their mother's father or *Nana*; each holds a specific station of love and veneration. There is a photograph of my *Dada* with his two sons and his eldest daughter in my mother's sitting room. He is in the typical attire that Muslim men wore in India during the early twentieth century, which is a long, fitted coat, with a banded collar hanging all the way down to the knees, the predecessor to the *sherwani* or tuxedo, which is worn even today by the Muslims of South Asia. In the photograph, *Dada* is wearing fitted pants loosely gathered at the ankles and a sculpted turban. His face looks stern, yet his hand around my aunt appears kind. My father always spoke about my *Dada* with a great deal of affection and with reverence, but with one exception, there were no anecdotes concerning him. What remains in my memory of *Dada* is the fact that he was a simple man who loved books, was principled and schooled in his convictions, and delighted in his two younger sons, my father and father's youngest brother, Nur usSalam (Light of Peace).

Very early in my life, my father took it upon himself to squash any pompous behavior I mustered towards my lineage. He impressed upon me that initially the title that had been given to my *Dada* was *Nawab*[2] or Lord and not *Khan Bahadur*, which is equivalent to a Baron. *Dada*, who really did not care much for British titles, took the opportunity to bargain for the governmental position of Assistant District Commissioner for his eldest son, Iskander Mohammed Salam, so that he too could serve his countrymen and better the lives of his people, especially the Muslims of Bengal. My father's eldest brother, Iskander *chach cha,* my eldest uncle, was already enjoying the rewards of earldom from *his* Nâna's estate and was not interested in earning the fruits of his labor. After a week in his newly acquired position, he stopped going to work and uttered the infamous statement that all us children have memorized when we did not want to do a chore: 'This job is not fit for the son of a gentleman.' I understand that my *Dada* never got over the humiliation, not because my uncle had insulted the British Government but because my uncle had refused to help his countrymen and, adding insult to injury, made his own father lose face in the bargain. My father made sure that I understood the ramifications of this episode: that it was my obligation as a member of my community to play a role in its betterment *and* to understand the significance of fulfilling Trusts given by parents on behalf of their children. I wanted to admire my uncle for what I wished to believe was his 'civil disobedience' towards the British Raj, but I learnt from his lifestyle that it was arrogance, not integrity, that made my uncle refuse to take that position. "A human being is remembered by the way he or she touches another member of the human race; the more you affect people positively, the more reason why your birth is a necessity to the world." This was my father's personal belief about each person's communal duties. Thus it was that, from that day, he painted into my consciousness a picture of arrogance that I named "*Iblis's* Achilles heel."

From my father I learnt the story of *Iblis's* fall from grace, a story that has affected me enough to determine my courses of behaviour even to this day. In the Quran, the story of *Iblis* – Lucifer of the Bible – is a very sad one. Early in my life I saw *Iblis* as the universal kin, the shared link by which each human being is connected to the rest of the human race, almost a reverse Adam connection. *Iblis*'s emotional outburst in that devastating moment when he, in impetuous willfulness, put all human beings' lives into mortal jeopardy was an act of a rejected child. His action was more a result of disappointment with himself than his hatred towards Adam. The only object that he could vent his frustration and shame towards were Adam and his progeny. In the Quran, *Iblis* was asked to acknowledge Adam by 'bowing' to him. Iblis refused, saying, *I am better than him (Adam), for I am created out of fire, while he is created out of clay.*[3] *Iblis* was elevated to the company of the angels even though he was not of them because of his great love for the Creator, but lost his social status with the Creator with that one act. Ultimately it was his ego or *nafs* that got in the way and contributed to his agonizing estrangement from what he loved the most. The story of *Iblis* is a tragic one for it paints two human failings: arrogance and spite.

From my father, I learnt that one great *jihad,* or struggle, in our lives is the struggle with our egos. Ego, I have realized, is the greatest seducer of all. It has a way of slinking into our unconscious and infiltrating our best of intended actions. My father made it a point to imprint in us all the iniquities that have ruined our family members. He never really spelled out '*Iblis's* Achilles heel,' but the more I have come to know myself, the more I have come to realize that I do have something in common with my wretched primal kin.

My *Dada* was the fifth-generation son of a Baghdadi religious scholar, who migrated from Baghdad to Delhi to perform *dawah* – religious education – during the mid-nineteenth century. The Bengal records of British India state that the Mughal Emperor Shahjahan asked *Dada's* great grandfather to move with his family from Delhi to Dhaka – then known as Shonargoan – the Golden City. In 1902, *Dada*, who was the Deputy Magistrate of Calcutta and known to the academic world as Maulvi Abd usSalam, authored the English translation of the book *Riyazu-s'alatin* – A Treatise on the History of Bengal – written by Ghulam Hossain Salem. It was the first documented history of Muslims in the Bengal region of India. My father, also a historian, pointed out that the significance of the book was not in its translation from the Persian book of the same name, but for the lengthy notes that accompanied the book. I was told that amongst *Dada's* peers, even though there was an in-house teasing that the length of the notes on each page of his translation equaled the length of the text, there was also an admiration regarding the scholarship, for the footnotes were of equal historical importance to the text. *Dada,* who had graduated from Calcutta University with a Master of Arts degree, had researched the notes to the text during his career under the British Raj. His mentor was the twelfth century Tunisian historian *Ibn Khaldun*, whose research methodology *Dada* used in gathering data for the notes to the book. My father, a historian of Islamic history, referred me to the works of this great explorer-historian when I too embarked on my graduate studies journey.

Prior to *Dada's* appointment as the District Magistrate of Calcutta he was the District Magistrate for the District of Faridpur, presiding out of the city of Faridpur. It was there that he heard of my paternal grandmother, Jannat-un-Nisa, and on a tenderhearted impulsiveness bordering on recklessness that defied logic or reason, married her. It is most assuredly a trait that has latched on to my genes, for *Dada's* decision to marry my paternal grandmother – *Dadee* – reveals an aspect of his personality that is quite out of character even for him. It is a legacy that I have inherited.

My *Dadee,* Jannat-un-Nisa, was the eldest daughter of Maulvi Gulam Ali Choudhrey, who was one of the three Muslim Landed Squires of East Bengal prior to the colonization of India by the British. He artfully dodged attention from the British by satisfying their hunger for money through payments of high taxes on these lands and earned the title of Choudhrey. My great grandfather, Gulam Ali Choudhrey, was in his sixties when he married my great grandmother, *Shundari Bibi* (Beautiful Lady). Word of her beauty had traveled and reached great grandfather's ears, and true to his character, he was determined to have her. We are told that he was a devoted and adoring husband, even though his tenantry accused him of ruthlessness.

Shundari Bibi's life reads like a story of a beautiful chaste maiden in her early teens who married the king of all the lands around her, only to have her devoted husband die in the fifth year of her marriage whilst in her second pregnancy, and be accused of adultery by her older step-children. Hers is also the story of a woman who at the age of nineteen decided to take her husband's entire family to court to fight for her and her children's right to their inheritance, an inheritance that was given to them by Islamic Law. *Shundari Bibi* was thirty-two years of age and still battling in the courts to prove the legitimacy of her younger daughter and her own integrity when her case was drawn at the Faridpur Court. My grandmother, *Jannat unNissa*, who had turned sixteen, joined her in these battles in the court and learnt very early to master the game of politics as well as manage the serfdom of the lands that she, her mother, and her eleven year old sister had inherited. *Dadee* was the only un-accused rightful owner of the properties that her father had left her family. She was a child bride, betrothed to the eldest son of *Zamindar* Monu Miah Choudhrey, whose lands comprised the Districts of Noakhali and Raipur, and was under his protection. Destiny, however, handed another twist to her life when her young husband died suddenly and Jannat joined the ranks of her mother and sister with no one to act as her ward.

In the Faridpur Court, the most scandalous case was that of the three beauties — Shundari Bibi and her two daughters. What was scandalous was the fact that the accuser was not the husband questioning the paternity of his daughter from his wife, but the deceased's sons and daughters from his first wife. I am told that the public were on Shundari Bibi's side. It could be because she came from their ranks and had climbed to her position due to her famed looks, or it could be because they held a quiet admiration for this audacious beauty, who was taking on the whole Choudhrey clan, single-handed.

It was around this time that Destiny joined hands with Cupid and my *Dada* entered the scene to hear the case of the three beauties. *Dada* was forty years old and widowed for the second time; he was not only getting over the untimely death of his second wife but was also struggling to be a single parent to his son and daughter from his first wife. Not only was the case rightly decided in favor of the three ladies, but *Dada* ended up marrying the newly widowed daughter. Why did he not marry Shundari Bibi, who was closer to his age than her sixteen year old daughter? Nobody really knows. He obviously did not speak of it to any of his children. I would like to speculate that Shundari Bibi was too spirited and *Dada* was looking for a less fiery, independent woman to mistress his home so that he could spend a great deal of time in the city (Calcutta) pursuing his academic career. Perhaps he thought that Jannat, a child widow who had matured early in life and had acquired a certain kind of street wisdom to handle her adversaries, would be the right person to raise his children. Perhaps *Dada* was a strong advocate for women's rights, for he had transferred these convictions to my father, who never failed to impress on me, from a very early age, that Muslim women had rights to property, money, and their own bodies sanctioned to them by God Almighty. There is a strong consensus that Dada, who wanted a large family, felt that Jannat was at the right age to fill the matriarchal shoes. Others said that *Dada*, who was extremely kind hearted when it came to women, feared for young Jannat's future. I think there is a possibility that he wanted a bride who would be forever grateful, independent enough to manage the household and let him pursue his academic career, and still provide him with a large family, since she was so much younger. We will never know.

My father never mentioned this menagerie of events, which was narrated to me by my father's first cousin two years after my father passed away. My father, on the other hand, has remained silent regarding much of his family's history. I am beginning to realize that there was a surreptitious side to father that we know nothing about, privy only to my mother. And that perhaps their relationship — which was tighter than friendship or spouse-ship, so much so that my father emotionally involved my mother in all aspects of his life — was a result of this knowledge. Did my father build his relationship with my mother as a kind of atonement for the loneliness his mother experienced, isolated in her estate in Haturiya, East Bengal, which she managed while *Dada* worked in Calcutta? I don't really know. I do know that my father could never separate himself from my mother in all his activities and that he adored everything that *Dada* was and stood for and held him up as an example for us to emulate.

An incident that has stayed in my mind pertaining to *Dada* is the one that my father repeated each time I made my yearly visit to see him — because it is the only story that my father has told me regarding his father. The event took place when *Dada* was very ill and nearing death. He had called for my father, who was studying at the University in Dhaka, to be with him during his last hours. *Dada* performed his last *wudu*[4] — ablution — by himself and changed into a fresh set of clothes in preparation for *salah* — prescribed form of prayer — as the late afternoon *adhan*[5] — call for prayer — had been called, and a short time remained for *salah*. At that moment the British Governor for Bengal, Lord Belvedere, came to visit *Dada* to pay his last respects. *Dada*, who had already performed his ablution and had prepared himself for what he suspected was his final worship, was not willing to associate in prosaic duties. With the following words he asked my father to request his excuse. "Tell his Lordship that your father thanks him for making the trip and regrets that he cannot meet him for he has already started the preparations to meet his Maker." "Why did he not meet him, isn't it Muslim etiquette to honor our guests?" I queried my father many times. Each time my father would look at me long and hard, disappointed in my question, and would ask me to reflect. "Your question is proof that you are not ready to hear the answer."

I never told my father that I had finally found the answer. Worship and prayer, I realize, are two different actions. Prayer can be done at any time, at any place, and in any form but *salah* or worship is an honored commitment to be performed at designated times in a form that has been entrusted to Muslims (in the *Quran*) by the Creator. These are specific moments in a day when Muslims are given the chance to make a point of connection with the Creator of time, space, and form. In the sacramental act of worship, a Muslim centrifugally goes through all the stages of creation from mineral, vegetable, animal, and human with the hope of connecting centripetally to her/his original self. Each of us at any given moment is awarded the gift to transcend time and place to arrive at a space where we may glimpse a reflection of Perfection. These are moments that may happen at unexpected times and/or within the discipline of everyday activities. However, the five prescribed times are openings to those moments. When *Dada* made preparation for what was his last mortal worship, he had opened up the walkway for the 'gift' to channel through to him and hence put every other obstruction aside.

My father repeatedly asked all of us children to acquaint ourselves with our ancestral heritage, and he would be disappointed if we could not quote from grandfather's book. It was the unspoken wish of my father that at least one of us would take up the challenge to write something that ambitious. That none of us did must have disappointed him. We will never know, for my father departed from us on the thirtieth of March, 2001 – the sixth day of Muharram, the first month of the Muslim year in the Muslim calendar year of *Hijri,*[6] 1422.

Since then, the long *gupchup,* or night chats, that I had with my father at his bedside have come to a close. The midday discussions over a bowl of blackberries and coconut water are now something to jealously cherish, for blackberries are no longer tempting and coconut water has gone back to being flat. It is yet one more chapter in my life's activities that has come to a close. Yet those nightly conversations filter through at odd moments and at the least expected times. Most persistent is the discussion about choosing a meritorious path. "Every course of action that is taken is from a choice that you make; learn to make the right choices." My father would quote accounts from the lives of people, including prophets from the Quran. He especially liked talking about the prophets Lut (Lot) and Ibraheem (Abraham) *(-AAS).* What he failed to mention was that they were extraordinary 'chosen' and 'guided' people. It was a deliberate omission since he believed that ordinary humans could elevate themselves to the ranks of the extraordinary. My father was convinced that each person was created with *barakka* or divine blessing and could, at any moment, reach out and act through it. I have tried to understand the significance of his words and connect them to some of the activities that he stressed, one of which is *salah* or worship.

The five daily worships for a Muslim and referred to as *salah* or *namaz* are about exercising the mind to reach a virtuous state. A virtuous state of being is about transmitting positive energy from the inner core of one's universal humanity to one's consciousness. The bodily movements during worship, the rhythm of the barely audible sounds and one's own life beat, all in perfect unison, have the power to open the blinds of inner vision so that the inexhaustible positive energy that is stored within finds release in meritorious acts. These released actions by their very nature are in perfect accordance with the actions of the Original Human and are positive actions since merit resides in the good and kind 'centers' of the true heart, and can be directed towards enlightenment.

In the Quran the Creator says, *I am closer to you than your jugular vein.* Are these 'centers' the portals into this closeness? I have come to believe that closeness to this Source results in meritorious acts, positive actions, and a frame of mind that is contained and at peace; whereas being separated from the Source results in being put in a place and on a path that is un-peaceful, the result of which is a state of discontent, unrest, and unhappiness. A contained heart at peace is a heart that is good, amassed in positive energy, and that has the ability to enlighten sentient beings through kindness. And it is this kindness that reflects back and in turn determines whether the chosen path in life is meritorious. Perhaps this is what my father meant when he said, "It is your heart that decides whether you will be at peace or discontented." Perhaps living life is not only about choosing how to drive around the curves but also about ascertaining the purpose of the drive. I hear his voice telling me that every course of action that is taken is from a choice made. Surely Life is a curved road. The challenge is never losing sight of the destination while interpreting and riding the curves as they come.

I believe my father's personal conviction had something to do with my developing awareness of accountability, so much so that it is a driving force in my behaviour and spills over into my painting process and philosophical investigations. Each mark that I make on canvas is an accounted mark, a burst of energy, made to sustain and connect with the next mark. Unconscious as it may seem, each mark nonetheless is a guided mark, a call waiting for a response. It is as though each painted mark is a protonic charge, so to speak, that hangs in space waiting to connect, through the power of its rhythm, to the next protonic charge. Conversations with my father also fueled the fire of my spiritual investigations and gave me an added drive to wring out of paint what may be considered the intangible. Art is about feelings, my father insisted. "Paint feelings through the objects but leave the objects far behind."

Of mutual interest to us both also was the subject of light. He would quote from the *Quran* chapter 24, verse 35, which states:

> *Allah is the Light of the heavens and the earth. The parable of His light is as if there were a Niche and within it a Lamp: the lamp enclosed in Glass, the Glass as it were a brilliant star: lit from a blessed Tree, an Olive, neither from the East nor the West, Whose Oil is well-nigh luminous, though fire scarce touched it. Light upon Light.*

This description of light as a metaphor for the radiance of the Creator is so expansive that my father would go into a rhapsody. At the end, his face would radiate like a beacon and everyone around him would be touched by this glow. I desperately wanted to paint the radiance of such feelings. Very early in my life, I looked in nature for life-forms that had the potential of radiating an energy field to which I could channel in and recreate through visual equivalents. Today I continue to look for "energy radiance" in all living things that are physical or metaphysical.

My father was an Honors student with a Bachelor of Arts degree in Islamic history and a historian who had the wisdom to translate academic and spiritual teachings into day-to-day practice. Only recently have I realized that he has been my invisible teacher throughout the time that I have lived and continue to live in the United States. What can be said of my father is that he was truly a beautiful, tenderhearted man, who radiated kindness. Fair in appearance and disposition, he was very principled, striving for the values instilled by his parents and encouraging the same in us. It is true that once you met my father you never forgot him for he had the ability to touch all who met him with great affection and radiance.

When I was eased into the profession of teaching Art in 1977, among the many factors that helped me develop my teaching philosophy were my father's words. I find myself teaching not just the technique and craft of my discipline – painting, but also developing in my students an aesthetic that does not advocate self-indulgence, and a perception about life that goes beyond the mere replication and narration of what is around us. I have also come to realize that Art is perhaps the only vehicle left today through which an individual can express a silent rebellion.

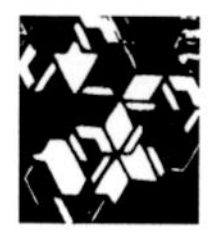

"Wom(a)n as home. The hearth of the joint family, the needle sewing its different members together. She is woman not only to her husband, but also to all the men of her husband's family, to her brothers, her cousins, and to her friends. She is equally mother of her children and mother of all the children of the family..."[7]

—Trinh T. Minh-ha

Mother Sun

My mother, Begum Fatema Reza, is the daughter of the late Ali Reza of Midnapore. My grandfather – *Nana* – was The Chief Residency Magistrate of Calcutta. Previous to that he was, during the Raj of the British in India, the Sub Division Officer of the Indian Districts of Jalpaiguri, Thakurgoan, Magura, and Comilla. The SDOs, as they were called, were very much like the Governors of our American states, and had a great deal of authority, as do our American governors. I remember him as small-boned, slight in frame, and quite frail.

My mother married my father in 1943 while still studying for her Masters degree, after graduating from Lady Brabourne College in Calcutta in 1944 with a Bachelor of Arts degree. She was a slip of a girl then, five feet one inch and weighing hardly 89 pounds. My father, who was a little over six feet, delighted in telling us 'stories' about their life together. The one he liked telling us the most is about the early days of their marriage during the British India period when he and *Ammi* – "mother" in the *Urdu* language – lived in a small rented flat off Nasiruddin Road in Park Circus, Calcutta, and took their daily evening stroll in the Grounds of Victoria Memorial. Prior to the partitioning of India, the grounds of Victoria Memorial were a favorite haunt of my great grandfather's family and my father, who was a grandson, was no exception. Exhibited inside the Memorial were painted portraits of the 'Sons of India,' one of whom was my *Dada's* father, Khan Bahadur Abdul Jabbar, known as Maulvi Abdul Jabbar because of his scholarship and linguistic abilities. He was fluent in Arabic, Persian, Urdu, Bengali and English, and was the Justice of Peace as well as the Persian Secretary to Lord Dalhousie, the Viceroy of India at that time. The Government of Calcutta later removed Abdul Jabbar's portrait after the division of Bengal into Hindu West Bengal, of which Calcutta was the capital, and Muslim East Bengal/East

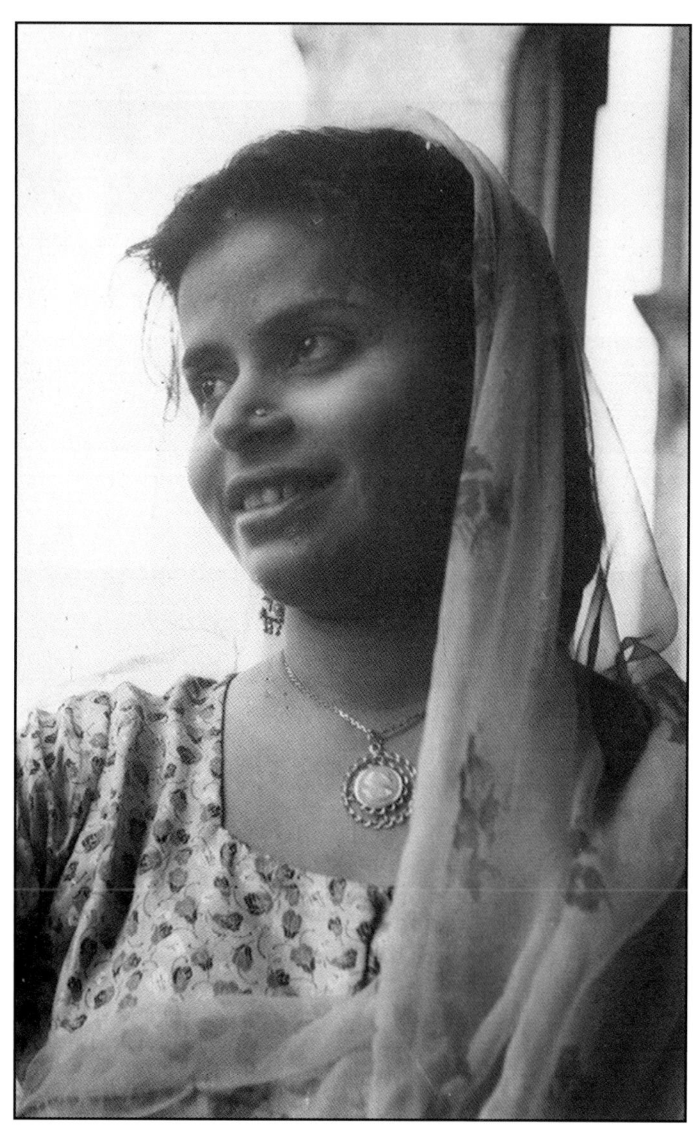

Pakistan (which today is Bangladesh) probably because he was a Muslim. My father never wished to speculate or discuss this incident, but it must have disturbed him deeply, for he never stood on Calcutta soil again.

My parents always referred to Calcutta as 'the City.' During all the time my brothers and I were growing up in East Pakistan, whenever my parents talked about 'the City' we knew they were referring to Calcutta. I was born in Calcutta after the infamous partitioning of India by the British, but I have not seen it since, even to this day. My father never wished to go back; it was a chapter in his life that he had closed. He banished Calcutta from his life as great grandfather Abdul Jabbar was banished from the annals of Calcutta history. The approach to life of leaving the past closed and of fulfilling the present is something, I believe, that is impregnated in my genes.

I learnt most about my mother from my *Nani* – my maternal grandmother – Rokeyya Begum. She preferred her grandchildren to call her *Ammijan*, which was unusual. A literal translation of the word *Ammijan* is 'mother of my life,' a word that is reserved for one's biological mother only. However, *Ammijan* was an unusual woman, and no one questioned her wish. She married my *nana*, maternal grandfather, at the age of fifteen, and bore him seven children. Like most middle class Muslim women of late nineteenth century India, she was educated in Quranic teachings in Arabic and Urdu in a strictly girls' *madressah*, or local school. After her marriage, my grandfather, aware of her sharp mind, hired a teacher to further her education in Urdu as well as in the English language. Ammijaan was an avid reader, and when no one was around, she would pick up our schoolbooks and go through them smiling quietly. The story that I like the best about my mother is told by *Ammijan*. It was about the time that my mother – *Ammi* – sneaked out both herself and her younger sister, my *khala* (aunt from mother's side) Rukhsana, who incidentally went on to become the first woman pilot of India, to attend a speech by Mahatama Gandhi at the Calcutta *Maidan,* The Indian Commons. My mother was seventeen years old and my *khala* barely fourteen. In those days, it was unheard of for girls from genteel Muslim families to go unchaperoned to any public meetings. Needless to say, my mother was in a lot of trouble but was bailed out as always by *Nana,* who encouraged his daughters to be adventurous

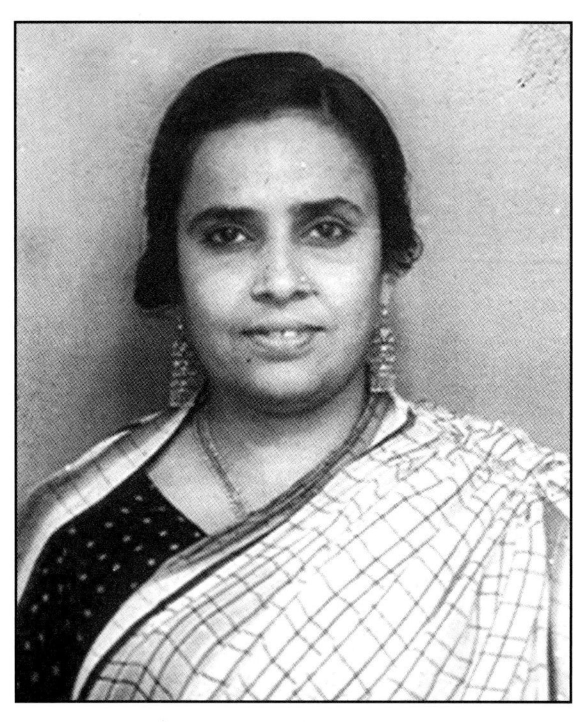

Ammijan, *Rokeyya Begum*

and have a free-spirited mind. There are stories of my mother and her sister Rukhsana attending the meetings of the Communist Party of India, better known as the CPI of Bengal. This organization, consisting of workers, peasants, middle class, and students, was founded in 1925 and was the new voice for the Indian masses. In the early forties, my mother and her younger sister rode on the new revolutionary wave that swept India in their struggle against the British Colonialists and Imperialism.

When I was a child, I marveled at my mother's spunk and would ask my grandmother over and over to tell me 'stories' about her. My grandmother would feign annoyance, but, with a twinkle in her eye, she would entertain me with stories of how my mother would get away with a lot of *shairarat* – mischief – and without doing her household chores, bury herself in 'her books' on account of what my grandfather would call her 'frail disposition.' "I knew that she wanted to get her hands on the books that your grandfather previewed prior to their release in the district schools." She chuckled with a quiet satisfaction whenever she spoke about my mother, for she had raised my mother with her own undaunted spirit and love for books. I am convinced that the same passion for reading has been passed on to me and is probably the reason why I have fought the computer as a reading tool.

I take pleasure in curling up with a book in odd places and at odd times. I like the immediacy of this warm and sensual object of information. The texture of paper is tactile and arouses a very physical experience that, when compounded with word abstractions, constructs solid images. I relish the smell of a newly printed book. The scent of the pages, reminiscent of the aroma of freshly baked pita bread, makes the book a delicious treat to hold. I enjoy the sound of the paper as I turn the pages and speculate its age from its worn face. I am intrigued by the many hands that have picked up the same book, for I can relate to their owners even though I don't know who they are. Sometimes the telling marks of food spilled on the pages can tell a story regarding what the reader was eating while reading. Sometimes bookmarks on a page and underlined words give you a clue as to what other readers were interested in. I share a book's vulnerability, for it reminds me of my own frailty. Each worn page is like the years of my own life. I hold the book with reverence, for it is an object that has carved its position into the physical world through its unique personality and message; it is as real as my own hand. I have traveled many times with a certain book tucked away in my purse to keep the accessibility of the written words close to my heart. They become magical presences endowed with an ability to transfer themselves into my consciousness.

Women in my family are like characters out of a story book, stirring my imagination as well as my personality. It was *Ammijaan* who told me about the women from my mother's side of the family, and instilled in me the kind of strength that I was able to draw on during the many harrowing times of my professional life. *Ammijaan* was the embodiment of the traditional Muslim woman, self-contained, unassuming, spirited, and sharply intelligent with an extended kindness that embraced all living things. There was a menagerie of domesticated animals and birds in her modest city residence. It was not unusual to wake up in the morning to the voice of Mittu the parrot crooning "Mittu my son wake up, wake up" and then try and race *Ammijan's* favorite dog Dopey to the hencoop to get a fresh egg for breakfast. I am convinced that my love for nature and animal life, especially dogs, is *Ammijaan's* legacy to me. Some of the best moments of my life were spent in the company of my two Weimaraner dogs, *Doee Raj* and *Rani Bibi,* and when they died I guarded their memory jealously, not willing to share those memories with anyone.

Ammijaan had a passion for growing things, especially all varieties of jasmine and gardenias. In winter when the jasmine shrubs would burst with flowers, she would string these flowers into garlands and wear them around her chignon and wrists. Even today, any contact with the flower or fragrance of jasmine can send me reeling through time back to the doorsteps of my childhood. It is she who taught me to look at plants very closely, distinguishing their fragrance and studying their shapes and color. She would give me names of different whites, one she would say is the color of *taaza makkhan* – fresh butter – another of aged butter or *purana makkhan*, and yet another of clarified butter or *ghee*.

I learnt very early to see variations and shades in the most subtle of hues and give them my own imaginative names. By recalling that particular name, I could visualize the hue. Even petals did not escape my grandmother's scrutiny. She drew my attention to the way petals of a flower fit into a circle or oval. When I would look at her in amused disbelief, she would chide me gently, telling me that I was not looking deeply into the language of nature. "Everything that lives exists within its own *halaqa* — circle — that is seen by your inner eye." She would place her finger on the part of my chest where my heart is located and say "By this! Close your eyes and open the ones that are locked in here." She would take the other hand and cover my eyes. This is my earliest recollection of art education. On reflection, I believe it is the base on which I developed my own color sensibilities and built my education regarding the physics of color, which ultimately led me to find new approaches in developing my own color theory and teaching color concepts.

My mother was my grandfather's pride and was known in my grandparents' very large family for her beauty and 'spirit.' In all the times that I was growing up, it was my mother's faith in my endeavors – never once bringing up my failings – that gave me the nerve to carry on with my pursuits. Pragmatist at heart, she has instilled in me her belief that if I never try, I will not know what I am capable of achieving. When I made the big jump to pursue painting as my lifelong pursuit, she behaved as though I had set out to practice this quest right from the start. She counseled me not to dwell on my actions as mistakes, rather to see them as bridges to be crossed in order to experience what is on the other side. She has a quiet way of accepting events that an average person may question. Never a pacifist, she is grounded enough to know when to choose her battles and win the war.

My father I liken to the moon, gone during the day only to return faithfully each night, bringing me a new face of beauty and excitement. I see my mother as the sun; her presence is constant, permeating and strengthening my actions, the source of my emotional comfort.

I remember a childhood nursery rhyme that my *ayah,* nanny, crooned when she took me out for a walk. It goes like this:

Chaand mama Chaand mama
Teep diye ja
Chaander kopale chaand teep diye ja
Uncle moon, uncle moon
Come touch this little one's forehead and leave
With the knowledge that you are caressing a moon-child.

The moon has been with me for as long as I can remember. As a child I slept to the sounds of the melody of my favorite moon-song and waited for the moon to appear each month, whole, shimmering in beauty. The deep colors of the night held a special significance and paralleled what my favorite song taught me. 'Sleep, sleep under the moonshine and the starlight, for the night is an ocean of honey.' It is only recently that I have put meaning to my relationship with nature's sun and moon. I am a sun-child hankering for the moon. Although the moon in the sky is a recurring source of inspiration, it is the sun that affects my moods and balances my psychological well being.

From a very young age I saw that my mother was my father's comfort emotionally, physically, and intellectually. In all the years that he was President of the Pakistan Chamber of Commerce, it was my mother who helped him write his speeches and accompanied him to various countries when he presented them. My younger brothers and I accompanied my parents only once to Istanbul, Turkey, in 1965. I have always known my father to be a self-assured man, a trait that I never could acquire, but I do believe that he grew taller when, during his presentation in Istanbul, I saw him steal a quick look towards my mother's direction and catch her give him a quiet smile. Theirs was a jostling relationship; they didn't agree most of the time. It was just that my mother had a different way of looking at life, and my father didn't always share those views. Many times I have witnessed their arguments, only to see my father come out of them with a bemused expression. I took that to mean that he was not really sure whether he had won the argument, for my mother had the wisdom of not arguing with my father, but would instead compliment him on his convictions and hold *her* ground, a practice that I have not acquired towards my husband. Unlike my mother, I have been occidentalized from a very early age to try always to get the last word in. It is a practice that has not served me well.

For my mother, my father was the anchor that held her steady as she went on destiny's course. She believed it was her providence to be bestowed with a demanding husband and four children and she met that challenge with fortitude, love, and an endless source of sacrifice. I do believe that it was through her determination and will that The All Pakistan Women's Association, of which she was the president, established in 1958 the All Pakistan Women's Association Girls High School in Chittagong, Bangladesh. It was my mother who carried the tireless task of collecting funds for running the school and a Children's Home on her tiny, five-feet one-inch shoulders without showing us the strain. Although, it must have been quite a strain to finance, run, and keep up the standards of both these institutions, and be a mother and wife. But my mother has the Reza toughness, a trait that has been endowed to all the five Reza sisters. Hers is a matter-of-fact toughness that can become quite rough at times. She has what everyone calls 'the look.' It has a way of making you squirm if you are caught in the act of not doing things right. Her intellect and her straight speaking intimidated even my father's friends; some of them, I do believe, were downright nervous of getting into a confrontation with her. When I was a young girl in middle school, an incident occurred that demonstrated to me very early in my life the moral character of my mother. My father had gone overseas for business, and one of his friends dropped in to visit us in the evening. Young as I was, I knew something was not right in the way he was speaking to her. I don't exactly know what my mother said, for she has never offered to give me an explanation, but I saw the gentleman almost fall off his chair, jump up, and hasten awkwardly out of the door. Even our butler, *Chand Meah,* was taken by surprise at his hasty departure. *Chand Meah* stood there with the tray of *naashta*, tea-snacks, in his hands, frozen to the ground, til he heard my mother calmly tell him to take everything back to the kitchen, adding that the guest was unable to stay. What my mother said to father's friend that night I do not know to this day. Many years later, after I was married, I thought I had earned the right to ask my mother what had happened that night. She gave me 'the look' and told me that it had not concerned me then and that still applied.

I believe I must have picked up some of her directness, for my reputation with my students is that I am a 'straight shooter,' calling it as I see it. This is my mother's legacy. I believe I have my father's pensive intelligence, my mother's hardheaded and independent spirit, and my very own trusting impulsiveness, laced with a ridiculous willfulness and an obsessive urge to always balance the scales.

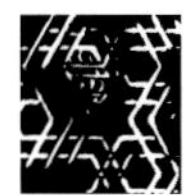

Travel in this life
Is through passages of Time
Each passage has a Station
Each Station a Departure[8]

— Quran

king of Salem (Salaam-Peace), acting as the eternal guide, leads young Santiago to his destiny, and it also explained my action as the act of one who had embarked on what I call destiny's roller coaster. Coelho says that 'mysterious forces' carry us on the path to what it is that we want for ourselves and that, if we truly want it, 'all the forces of the universe conspire' to help you achieve it.[9]

So I bade goodbye to my soup cans, giant hamburgers, Coca-Cola bottles, and all the subject matter of the seventies for which I had no taste, feelings, or melody. I had questioned then the relevance of why soup should be cooked and put into a tin can to be eaten a few months or days later. Convenience, yes, but it never tasted as good as fresh. Why eat something just to eat and why paint something just to paint, I asked, and why was the tin of soup considered so 'beautiful' and relevant a subject matter for painting? I had asked the question then and was told that beauty was not part of the contemporary painting equation. Art was about the present, about now, about what we did, about popular culture, about everyday genre; the idea of the sublime in art was no longer relevant. Today I believe that my questions were answered in the form of Art Professor Elmer Schooley's invitation to come study with him. It was one of the 'mysterious forces' at play. Little did I know then that New Mexico would be where I would come to acknowledge my inner shadow-friend.

The relevance of making art and, in my case, painting, has always been an important issue to me. Why paint if it is not to touch the sublime? What is the sublime? A feeling? And what is this feeling about? Is the sublime feeling as evasive as the truth we seek about ourselves, and can it be captured in paint? More important, is the sublime feeling transportable to another human being through what the aesthetician Clive Bell calls the 'significant form?' What makes form significant; what are its inherent qualities? Clark Hetherington refers to a well-told story as having a 'fascinating form.' Are both of these scholars talking about the same thing? I still struggle with these questions, for this line of questioning that started in Las Vegas, New Mexico, has stayed with me throughout my life, directing and shaping the content of my work.

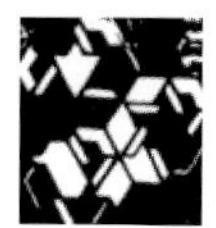

"Truly in the body there is a morsel of flesh which,
if it was whole, all the body is whole
and which, if it was diseased, all of it is diseased.
Truly it is the heart."

— Prophet Mohammed (AAS)

"The heart is between two of the fingers
of the All-Merciful."

— Ibn al-'Arabi

Nature Passage

Las Vegas, New Mexico, in 1972 was a town cut off from city time. It was not a sleepy town severed from the rest of American civilization, it just operated within its own rhythmic course. As the bus dropped me off at the foothill of New Mexico Highlands University, I can recall a dazed young girl looking around, willing someone to transport her to the door of the Admissions Office. There was only one major street then, and this street, which wormed its way and serviced the town of Las Vegas, was deserted. It was high noon right at *Dhohr*[10] time, when the sun bestows shadows that are exactly the same length as the objects. The street wound its way up to the top of the hill like a silent rattlesnake, but the top of the hill chimed with voices. This was my first conscious initiation to the paradox of simultaneity. I had traveled thousands of miles to this sparsely populated hill station to be taught the first important lesson in my new journey, that all things carried within themselves their own growth and extinction.

I started my journey to the top of the hill with my metal trunk, which housed everything I owned from personal belongings to art supplies. The trunk probably weighed 50-60 pounds. Compared to my then 90-pound frame, it could have been an impossible task to lug my worldly possessions all the way up. But that's what I did. I picked the trunk up by its side handles with both hands and, with my back to my destination, I started up the road. I was excited. I knew I would get to the top and that everything was as it should be. Even at this early period in my life, I knew *something* would happen if I started the *something ball* in motion. I know now that insight is a glimpse into Providence. When one is young, the perception of wondrous phenomena are easily acceptable as one has a more trusting heart. Maybe it is because one wills it with a sincere and believing heart. As one grows older, there is that gnawing voice of cynicism that edges its way in and blocks the 'miracle'[11] from stepping in; and a miracle did come that day on Main Street of Las Vegas in the form of a dusty, grey-blue truck that carried me to the top of the mountain. Thus I began my second childhood in seeing, hearing, touching, tasting, and, above all, feeling.

I stayed in New Mexico Highlands University from 1972 to 1973 and graduated with a Master's degree in painting and drawing. Even today my memories of my graduate days cannot be separated from my memories of New Mexico. It was a period of quiet and of rejuvenation. New Mexico was my sanctuary. The war years of 1970 and 1971 in East Pakistan, later Bangladesh, and the bewildering years at Columbus College of Art and Design seemed distant. My mother was safe in England along with my two younger brothers, and my father in newly formed Bangladesh was the only one to worry about. And worry I did, but the brilliant blueness of the New Mexican sky was a shining canopy that lit my space with compassion and hope. The New Mexican blue is unequal to anything blue that one can visualize. It is clearer than glass and sharper than ice. It has the freshness of morning dew and the brightness of the afternoon sunlight. It is truly a blue that one has to experience and, once experienced, it imprints itself into one's DNA. I have carried this blue with me and once in a while it manifests itself in my paintings. It appears in my paintings out of nowhere to reassure me when I have doubts about myself and my pursuits. I have been asked by my students about the formula of this blue in my paintings and I have found that the colors that I use, cobalt, manganese blue, cerulean and ultramarine blue, do not result in this azure-like sky blue: for the New Mexican blue results from the application – the scumbling, peeling and the layering of all these blues – and appears as a gift for solace.

My lifestyle in New Mexico heightened my *instinctabilities* – a word I coined similar to sensibilities but suggesting instinct awareness and receptivity. I became a turtle that could trace out the innate markings on the breast of the earth to form the mountains in my landscape. And, like the coyote, I found myself smelling out the fragrances of immanent colors in the sky. The land was teaching me to paint through a heightened sense of instinct. I experienced an excitement that I had not experienced before. Is this what Vincent Van Gogh experienced when he traced the planetary rhythm around the stars, in the painting *Starry, Starry Night?* What about Vincent's apple trees! Was I brought to New Mexico to find fields of these trees and sense the celestial rhythm? It was not déjà vu, nor was it a continued bonding with Vincent Van Gogh — one that had started in the summer of 1965 in Paris — for I painted as though programmed. I spent hours outside alone, walking, hiking, and simply basking in the heat of the sun like a curled up copperhead or daydreaming, all to an awakened instinct regarding trails, spaces, and resting places. The whole time I lived the life of a naturalist I never encountered rattlesnakes, bears, or scorpions. Perhaps I was lucky or perhaps in this 'outback' my instinct to survive was in its highest form. Or better still, I had tuned myself into the workings of nature and was under her protection. At least this is what I would like to believe.

I found balance in the New Mexican landscape. The blue symmetry of the sky is in total proportion with the burnished gold of the expressive forms on the ground. I had found my teacher in nature. However, it was not just color that I was learning from the New Mexican natural environment. I was learning to look at nature with a different eye, an eye turned inwards. At times, the light outside was so blinding that my eyes would tire, and in tiring, the actual vision of the environment would change into a field of miniscule fragments of light matrices. The mesas would no longer appear as large jutting pegs stabilizing the expanding desert, but as very intimate sentries, dissipating into infinitesimal particles of a zillion musical hue particles. Colors blazed on my canvases as I tried to put down these marks of colors. I would learn much later that what I was seeing without realizing were particles of my own origin. There is a passage in the Quran that reads: *And we created Adam out of clay and breathed into him Our Spirit.* I believe today that I was in the early process of making a connection with my primordial innocence.

I know now that I was privileged to get a glimpse into the very nature of earth itself, for the congealed dust that is New Mexican ground is a study in patterns. The fissures in the ground take on a rhythm that is shared by the riverbeds, and the gorge. Even the pine trees and the ground have a way to stay in their own place and at the same time reach and touch the sky. I know now that what I was experiencing then is the unity in creation, masterminded by a divine plan, and that The Planner has instilled within us the ability to grasp this knowledge, if we should choose to understand it as such.

As a child, I was an avid gardener delighted by the sensuality of color, texture, and fragrance, but in New Mexico, intuition prevailed over mindsets regarding visual perceptions, technique, and aesthetics, and I came to feel my connection with the earth, the soil, and the beauty of its composition through the geometry of color-forms.

Intuition is a sudden immersion of the soul into cosmic memory where the record of all the histories of people, places, and beings are written as one smooth current of connections. Intuition is tapping into this 'record'; it is a pipeline into the universal language. I remember reading a piece of advice given by a sage to his student, in which the master asked his student to relax the mind and learn to 'swim' in order to escape from the mind's confusion. Sheikh ad Darqawi, a Muslim sage of the twentieth century, explains confusion as *hayrah,* a mental state in which the mind comes up against its own limit and, in a sense, is overloaded with information. In New Mexico I started my journey in 'letting go.' It was not so much that I had developed the ability to intuit but rather it was the beginning of releasing precepts. One 'intuits' when for a split moment the mind blanks out of its information mode and goes on automatic. It is a moment of complete 'sight' and awareness and, in a sense, timeless. To me it was the closest I could come to a sublime experience.

I have an urge to capture the moment of complete 'sight' and manifest it in a form that will convey the visual expression of this moment, for if sublime is the pinnacle of elation, this moment surely is *it*. As an artist I search to become independent from a state of *hayrah*, or what I call mind-bewilderment. I want to be more than a storyteller, a narrator, a recorder or a surveyor and, above all, I wish to rise beyond the traditions of cultural information that is stored within me and enter a realm where imagination, feelings, and insight fuse to show a clarity of vision of the world(s) in which I exist.

I have read that people can ensnare you with their charm; Homer knew of this; why else did he repeatedly introduce the sirens? Perhaps Homer's sirens were a metaphor for a sense of place rather than persons per se. The sailors in the *Odyssey* were enchanted with the lore of the place, so much so that they forgot all sense of acquired perception with regard to time and place. A similar yet different time-place notion is in the sentiment expressed by the Indian, Mughal Emperor Shah Jehan, when he encountered the magical landscape of Kashmir. His immortalized exclamation of that first meeting, "if ever there is a heaven on earth, it is this, it is this, it is this," has been forever imprinted on the walls of the *Diwan i Khas* in Fathipur Sikhri, India, and in the hearts of the literati of the Indo-Pak sub-continent. Seduction comes in many forms. It may hit you through your senses, but there are other moments when it passes your immediate senses and hits you in the core of your heart, awakening memories within your collective mind of places you have been and of beauty you have experienced. It is like *déja vu* but of a more powerful nature. The mesas, the desert, and the mountains of New Mexico had cast a net from which I had no desire to escape.

In the New Mexican landscape of magic I was spellbound in an unrequited disquiet, captivated, for I did not know how to move in and out of the world of my inner sojourns. At times, I could faintly visualize wondrous landscapes but could not manifest them in paint. I just did not have the tools. So I painted not so much concerned with what I was achieving, but working the process in the hope of reaching the magical space of my senses. I was simply painting. I painted morning, noon, and night, at odd times and during weekends, always outside, never in the studio. There was so much to listen to in the desert. In the mountains of Montezuma, New Mexico, I listened to the way the pine trees moved; there was music, and with it rhythm. I painted these rhythms into patterns of forms, and what I could not, I imprinted into my heart for I was conversing with nature; it was an art conversation. Like nature, I simply became a maker of forms. This is the legacy of New Mexico.

The newfound patterns that manifested as linear rhythmic brush marks in my New Mexican canvases, whether I painted landscape, barrios or downtown Las Vegas, stayed buried in me to crystallize into independent patterns that I refer to as shape-forms in my 1985 Uniscape canvases. Later, in my 1990 canvases, there was yet another development, trees, rivers, mountains, plains and houses all subordinated themselves to the *rhythm* of these matrices.

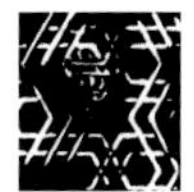

And when I love Him
I am the ear with which He hears
And the sight with which He sees
And the hand with which He grasps
And the foot with which He walks
— Prophet Mohammed

The Knowledge Passage

I was closing the chapter to my American experiences and starting on my return to Bangladesh when once more I rode the surf of the 'mysterious force.' In 1974 Texas was the biggest exporter of raw cotton to Bangladesh, and my father was one of the main importers. He was invited to Lubbock, Texas, to meet with the American traders, and I was to accompany him. On an impulse, I enrolled as a Ph.D candidate in Fine Arts at Texas Tech University and started on a yet more complex journey in painting. If my experience with the elders at the Navajo and Pueblo villages in New Mexico is where I re-learned to find my human heart, in Lubbock, Texas, I was to find my buried intellect. My education in Lubbock had more to do with exploring kindred minds, and through my readings, I discovered kindred spirits who spoke to me – heart to heart. I was immersed in a form of education in which new mind centers were awakened to query.

I studied books by such authors as Henry Corbin, Titus Burchardt, Rene Guenon, Syed Hassan Nasr and Martin Lings, all of whom reaffirmed and explained the writings of historical scholars in a way that reciprocated my feelings regarding nature. It is said that one responds only to what is already within oneself; thus began the passage through hidden portals to un-tapped revelations that spoke to me through varied voices.

Nature *is* alive, having its own intelligence; it makes decisions and transforms. Everything in nature speaks through its own language. Trees communicate with the earth; landmasses make decisions for themselves whether to stay hidden or fixed or to split open. Trees cry when cut down, rocks scream when pulverized and water weeps when it is made to turn rancid. I learned that the human mind has the capacity and sensitivity to see, to hear, and to feel the joy and anguish of all living forms. It was all about learning the languages of nature. My perception developed further in the understanding that all living things coexist in accordance to a pact, and that we humans are the only ones that stray away and live outside that pact.

In Lubbock I was also initiated into the theory of self-disclosure by philosophers such as Muhyuddin Ibn Arabi, Rumi, Imam Gazzali, Semnani, and Leonardo Fibonacci. From Fibonacci I learnt that there was a ratio of measurement that enlightens everything living. I studied Leonardo Da Vinci's illustration of Luca Pacioli's dissertation, which informs us that the human body also grows in a ratio of proportion similar to some of the life forms of nature. The knowledge of a Divine Planner having a hand in all of this became a reality. This thesis ran parallel to my past education and awakened me to the understanding that the religion of Islam conveyed the message of acknowledging a Divine Order within which each created atom plays a significant role. For the first time I began to see a glimpse of my relationship to this Order as I lived outside my national cultural box in a state of inner transformation. I was riding the surf of Elise Boulding's 'axial ages,' going through periods of transformation, sharing the sensibilities of great minds, and gaining new understanding about myself in relation to my environment and feelings. Bolding suggests that the new millennium "is a historical time where people, ideas and cultural traditions from widely different regions interact with one another in a sustained manner. At such times there is a flowing of human creativity as people generate new understanding and develop shared sensibilities." The more sure I became of this revelation, the more my paintings suffered. I could not reconcile what I experienced with what I was learning. I tried to paint the new information into my visions of nature and failed. I was trying too hard, so I stopped painting and allowed myself to drift in this stream of learning.

It was the remarkable teacher Cerno Bokar's statement, "The light of Truth is darkness more brilliant than all the lights combined" that challenged me to look for visual color from sources other than sight alone. Bokar's spiritual insight had penetrated the realm of science far earlier than the physicists of the twentieth century, who explained the expansion of the universe in terms of dark matter transforming into space matter, energy, and motion. Bokar's insight is through his reflection of the Quranic verse, *I create creation and repeat it.* Bokar echoes the idea that the hidden – *zahir* – (the dark) has more 'energy' (light) than all the light (energy) that exists around us, and that the concept of Truth is constantly in motion, evolving, getting larger – like the universe – as we as individuals evolve spiritually.

I looked for other forms of visible color through art disciplines such as metal enameling, glass-blowing, weaving, and surface design, and immersed myself with different processes that enrich one's vision about color, besides paint. I began to incorporate the elements of fire, air, and water into the painting process. Heating metal and hammering out its form gave the metal a lustrous hue that was both elusive and iridescent, and thus capable of creating the illusion of three-dimensionality on the surface of the metal, without the need for hue-blending or modeling. I developed transparency in color by firing colored glass using a process known as enameling and acquired a new understanding of how heat and fire can act as catalysts in the processes of change and transformation. I saw that a simple process such as firing glass particles in high heat on metal could transform the surface of the metal and endow it with a skin of shimmering color. I was captivated by the alchemy of enameling and sought to introduce a technique in oil painting whereby opaque paint could alter its physical chemistry, leaving behind encrustations of transparent color on the surface of the canvas.

I began to look for a common thread that would connect all the processes in making a painting without regard to subject matter or content. I simply worked the various processes, learning from the different art disciplines regarding form, structure, and technique and applying the visual qualities of one to another. As for content, I did not know how to express it all through my paintings, so I buried it. A new spark had been ignited in terms of how I was looking at and experiencing the world around me. I simply kept my eyes open and the fire of information burning within. Out of this new-found working mode emerged an appetite for self-discovery and a fusion of hand and sight.

But it was such thinkers as Henry Corbin, Titus Burchardt, Rene Guenon, and Syed Hassan Nasr, who pushed me to ponder the spiritual side of my temporal existence. I saw myself as an inhabitant of the Garden of Eden, sent to this Planetary Garden with an unverbalized mission and an implant telling me how to act in harmony with other life-forms of this planet. The implant was my conscience; some refer to it as instinct. When one is heedless to this voice, there is an intervention from the Master Voice – the Voice of Guidance. I recalled the term 'alien' used by the U.S. Immigration Office for a non-citizen. Surely an alien is one who lives outside the Planet Earth's cycle, in awe of nature's actions, in love with nature's beauty but with an innate urge to dominate and ultimately vanquish what may appear strange and incomprehensible.

The cultural climate that I had created for myself in Lubbock, Texas, put me in the right frame of mind to study Ibn Arabi's book, *Journey to the Lord of Power*. Books such as this are known in the Anglo-European west as Sufi literature; however, in my parents' home they were never referred to as 'Sufi' literature. They were simply books by devout Muslim thinkers who were practicing the fundamentals of Islam in the most humanly perfect way, and whose love for the Creator had reached such heights that they became infused with the transmission of Islamic practice and served as guides for those who were on a quest for the virtuous, dimensional side of Islam.

Sufism is understood in the west as the mystical dimension of Islam and is separated from what the west calls "mainstream" Islam; however, that is very misleading and perpetuates division among Muslims and non-Muslims regarding the breadth of the religion of Islam. People who were and are on the path of *Tassawuf* were known later in history as Sufis, men of the "*suffa*." These individuals, under the exemplary practices of the prophet Mohammed *(-AAS)*, acquired a higher level of devotional piety than other Muslims, and drew Muslims from all over the Muslim world looking for instructions in sanctity. Informal schools in the form of *halaqa* (circles) formed around these teachers, which through the centuries became more structured and individualized, and in time acquired the name of *zawwiya* (Arabic), *tekke* (Turkish), and *dergah* (Persian). For people on this virtuous path, or *tariqa,* it is a way of functioning, in that every cognitive act of realizing one's place in the terrestrial realm is in accordance with the directives of the Supreme Being. Thus people on the path of *tassawuf,* such as Sheik Muhiyuddin Ibn al 'Arabi, Imam Gazzali, and Shahbuddin Yahya Suharwardi, whose books I was reading at that time, are also known as 'People of Light.' People of Light have conquered ignorance to walk in knowledge. Strict in their observances of the Quranic shariah, they have recognized it as rungs of a ladder that can take them to the eye of the Great Light and, because of this recognition, have been blessed by the Creator of the Universe and brought forth from the shadows of ignorance into the light of knowledge. Taking to heart the dictums of the prophet Mohammed *(-AAS) to be in the world, but not of it*, these individuals recognize the signs and reflection of the Creator in every atom of the Universe and thrill in exalting the Creator in their daily action. Reading these books, I thrilled. The sleeper had awakened to reexamining beliefs that lay dormant.

Foremost in my books was the Holy Quran. I realized that the Quran was a book of signs, and that within each verse there was a signal for the intellect. Lives of the Quranic prophets were lighthouses to guide searching individuals in their pursuit for self realization. I learned that self realization came when trusted authority was handed over to one's Benefactor in order to ignite one's intuitive and intellectual abilities – to acquiesce to the benevolence of the trustee. I learned that trust was to completely abandon oneself in the trustee's love. The story that affected me a great deal was that of the prophet Ayub (Job) *(-AAS)*. If there is an example of one hundred percent devotion to one's beloved, surely it is in the example of this trusting man towards his Creator. I memorized Ayub's supplication that children in Muslim countries are taught very early in their lives: *My Beloved Lord, distress has afflicted me but you are the most merciful of mercies* (Al-Quran).

In times of utter despair these imploring lines can bring great solace. I recognize that peace is an outcome of an inner reflection that occurs when one allows oneself to be totally consumed by the embrace of the Soul Maker. Hence the Quranic verse, *Peace, a Word from God, a Lord most Merciful.*

I was drawn to biographies of regular men and women scholar/sages as well. The ones who particularly interested me were Pythagoras, Muhiyuddin Ibn 'Arabi of Andalusia, and the Poet Rabi'a al- Adawiyya of Basra. It seemed books fell into my lap. I would read a book only to find a particular name pop out and light up. I would then become a somnambulist in search of ways of getting information on that person from books written by and about that individual.

Much later when I mentioned these writers to my mother, she smiled and said "*Amma* (mother) was right after all." *Ammi* had read many books by these authors while she was pregnant with me. My grandmother, *Amejaan*, whose spiritual education was formed in the *madrasa* school system, had impressed upon *ammi* that a baby's learning starts while still a fetus and that everything a mother observes, reads, sees, hears, and tastes is transmitted to the child within. *Amejaan* insisted that a mother's eyes, ears, nose, and mouth are portals and the information that passes through them remains forever in the child's consciousness. Perhaps the fact that my mother read 'enlightening books' and had pictures of beautiful babies surrounding her during her pregnancy accounted for why I was drawn to these books. However, that is stretching the illogical thread, because *Amejaan's* theory worked only in parts. As a baby, I did not come up to my maternal grandparents' expectations in appearance and was considered to be a very ordinary looking child.

In Lubbock, Texas, my best friend was the Interlibrary Loan librarian. Unlike today, it was necessary to fill out reference forms and justify the need for books acquired through this system. The librarian would question me as to why I needed that book, especially the ones which had to be brought from overseas libraries. 'What do these books have to do with art?' the librarian would ask. 'I don't know,' I would reply. 'I have lost my way, and one of these books will have the answer.' My answer must have amused her because from then on she referred to me as "the lost scholar."

My readings prodded a direction I had never considered, the impact of sounded words on human physiology. I recalled words of my voice instructor, *Ustad* (Master) Wilayat Ali Khan, elucidating that the body was a vessel very much like a *tabla*, a hollow Asian drum. He explained that some sounds, when practiced correctly, could make the whole body resonate, unifying all levels of one's consciousness and forging the possibility within the body of producing a synchronized music of a universal nature. This I recognize today to be music consciousness.

Ustad never tired of retelling the story of *Tansen,* the legendary Indian musician who controlled natural phenomena with his singing. *Tansen* spent most of his time in the natural habitat of animals for melody inspiration. It is said that his singing brought down rain and lighted fires.

One story is that while watching birds in the jungle at dusk, *Tansen* observed a flock of birds singing in the primordial style of call and response. At a certain pitch, a unison of musical notes set the twigs on fire. *Tansen* memorized the notes and after much experimentation and formulation turned the notes into a *raga,* the *raag* Deepak. In classical Indian music *raag* refers to an acoustical method of arousing the senses and feelings of the listener. Hence the *raag* consists of qualities that include a modal structure with the potential to escalate and diminish movements which ascend and descend a prescribed number of notes and a distinctive scale within which melodies may be developed.

Tansen was a virtuoso of *Kheyal,* the Indian version of opera, and when he performed the Deepak, we were told, fires lit up all around him. Akbar, the Great Mughal emperor of India, would have unlit lamps in and all around his palace to show off the musical power of his great protégé. However, as in all legends, no story is complete without the proverbial battle of good versus evil, with good triumphing in the end. So in this tale, intrigue within the palace led rivals of Emperor Akbar to force Tansen to sing the *Deepak Raag* and light fire to the properties all around the emperor's grounds. But good triumphs, and *Tansen's* brilliance as a musician shines in the way he outwits the emperor's rivals in the form of a counter *raag*, the *raagni,*[12] *Megha Malhar,* which *Tansen* composed and taught to one of his contemporary female singers in order to counteract the resonating energy of the *Deepak.* At the legendary occasion when Tansen performed the *Deepak* and fires started burning properties, his lady friend immediately started singing *Megha Malhar*, which brought rain clouds and doused the fires. Such was the power of the celebrated Tansen, the genius who could alter the course of nature with his *ragas*.

What has always impressed me about legends is the creative magnitude of the human mind to construct complex structures that expand the spiritual dimension of humans, endowing them with abilities that lie quietly smoldering under the coals of daily activities. Do legends have an atom of truth to them? How do legends get started in the first place and why? The answer to that could probably be in the fact that there are different forms of legends. Tansen's is most probably a mythological legend; however, there are traditional legends that are of a historical nature, such as the one that is taught to Muslim children in Africa, regarding the power of the sound of the word AL LAH, – The One – in which four letters are enjoined to *read* as three, *sound* as two and *make* one word. In an old Mali tradition, Muslim children are taught:

> "Write the divine name ALLAH on a wall, in front of your bed, so that it may be the first image offered to your sight on waking (REMEMBRANCE). Invoke it fervently (*dikr*) from the depth of your soul, so that it may be the first word coming out of your lips and striking your ear. At bedtime, fix your eyes on it so that it may be the last image you contemplate before you subside in the temporary death of sleep. If you persist, in course of time, the light contained in the secret of these four letters will spread on you and a spark of the Divine Essence will set your soul on fire and will radiate it."

The two cases cited are similar in their utilization of light, illumination, and energy, but that is where the similarity ends. The theory behind the light energy in Tansen's case is of a pyrokinetic nature; it is a result of a metaphysical source of narrow and focused energy unleashed, working parallel with Tansen's sound frequencies, and synchronizing with the frequency of the oil in the lamp, in order to make the oil resonate to the extent that, at a certain resonance level, the vibration produces combustion. Malian light, on the other hand, is the result of an inner combustion. In the second case, a metaphysical energy focuses the sound waves to synchronize with the body's cellular atoms, electrified to the point that each protonic entity in the human body is in a state of vibrational unison. It is energy level in the body at its highest point *and* in perfect harmony with the body's temperature. This is what I understand to be a mystic experience: an experience of transmutation, where body, ego, and spirit find a kinship with the soul, for it is the soul's energy that drives the mind and body to this spiritually heightened state.

Henry Corbin, in his book *People of Light,* tells us that Najm Kobra, the thirteenth century Muslim mystic, described mystic experience as an "intimate feeling that an event is taking place within you." Intimacy implies closeness. This closeness is an interfacing of the senses, the blending and bleeding of the physiological senses, arousing within the self's 'new life' an acute awareness. It is a state of total synchronization of body, ego, spirit and soul. The 'event' that he mentions is the inner combustion, the body in full, attentive knowledge of its soul. These are people of light, whose actions are guided by supra-sensory organs that exist outside the normally understood physiology of the human body and produce 'senses' from dimensional planes that exist and function outside linear time patterns.

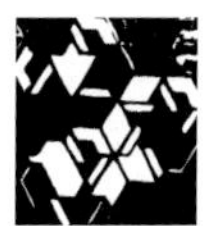

"Time as you know it will pass into timelessness . . . Be conscious; take advice from what you see. Listen to your conscience and talk with reason. . . . Speak gently to ignorance. Be quiet and polite in the presence of wisdom . . . . The purpose of your coming to this world is to know yourself and to know the truth."

— Kaygusuz Abdal
Budala-name

The Tunnel of Afflicted Existence

There is a period in my life that is difficult to share even with myself. It is neither an era of regret nor an era of mistake but a period of an inner struggle. A self-imposed exile is a walking hybrid, a chameleon that changes to what it perceives its social environment calls for. In 1977, I was that being. I moved in and out of dense holes of darkness. The canvas of my life was a Futurist painter's worst nightmare. People, events, cultural values and time were compressed into a homogenous continuum in which I functioned in total alienation from my spiritual self. Even my shadow had abandoned me in total disillusionment.

Like a painter scraping paint from a canvas that is saturated with muddy paint, I made a decision to scrape my life of its excess baggage, to start anew. It was perhaps the most desperate action I have ever taken, for in sealing the doors to certain chambers of my life that were disquieting, I risked losing the wellsprings that had nourished my psyche and prompted me to where I was at that time. There were no guarantees that these self-imposed seals could be broken open again. It would be many years before I was able to find new doors to revisit them.

In September of 1977, a door opened, and I walked through it, my shadow and I, to a town in the middle of the Appalachian mountains of Virginia. It is, today, 30 years ago.

Radford, Virginia, is a town very much like the *Hotel California* described by the rock group The Eagles in their song, for once in Radford it is difficult to ever leave. There is a charming complacency within the town which feeds the University holding the same name. The town is unique in that it grows with new inhabitants without visibly growing in numbers. New shops on Main Street replace old ones and even with a face lift, the less than one mile long street remains pretty much intact in its sameness. It is as though one arrives in Radford and begins a process of transformation to become a Radfordian, shedding one's dreams and visions to accommodate the university-town. I knew, when I got there, that I could ease myself into this new role, yet in trying to do so, unwittingly I had started my passage through what Edward Sayeed refers to as the 'tunnel of affliction,' a passage through which there is a kind of distancing from one's soul.

My shadow mocked and pulled away each time I tried to settle down into the life of a Radford professor. Although I was a painter, I was hired as a textile instructor and assigned to teach in almost all other areas of art but painting. It was a general understanding in the art department that a terminal degree in art automatically gave one the credential to teach in *all* areas of art. Disengaged from what I knew best, I plunged into a state of confusion.

Nature came to my rescue once more. Perhaps it was because of the pact we had made, but I like to believe it was something more. The human body, in its chemistry, is tied to the earth's substratum and energy and to the moisture in the air. My eyes opened to the forms of flowers, to the rhythm in the petals, to sounds and fragrances. The rolling indigo mountains, the smoky azure sky and the dull greenery lulled my senses and rocked me into a state of stupor in which the expansive and enlightening experience of New Mexico and Lubbock, Texas, surfaced to ride in a single surf. My eyes opened to the commonalities living things share with each other, and I sought to paint it through the structure of nature forms, and through geometry.

I went back to Euclidian geometry, this time to penetrate the equations and constructions and to apprehend 'the point' as the origin, the Ultimate Source, the beginning of the infinite whole, divisible and complete. In relating the point to the source of nature and the universe at large, I looked for harmonious divisions to become the symbolic expression of Tawhid – The Metaphysical Doctrine of Divine Unity, and my drawings and paintings its geometric expressions. I saw nature as a terrestrial web, structured with set boundaries within which shapes turned to forms, colors lay to overlap and lines wrapped, stretched, and faded. Each unit of the web was a living consciousness, complete, divisible, and harmonious with the next. Could these universal landscapes that I was painting be a reflection of a unity that I was experiencing? Was this *Wahdah,* the Unity that deals with the concept of a nonspatial existence of reality, of existence in one dimension? And was it possible to relate our consciousness with the consciousness of the material world? Was I relating my perceptions with my non-conscious dimensions as well as the dimensional world simultaneously, and in so doing, was I creating a canvas that was a fusion of these realms?

I cannot be that presumptuous. Perhaps it was simply another form of déja vu. In the patterns and rhythms of the trees, lichens, water, and rocks, I saw a sequential but independent order that acted with the order of the universe. It was a different rhythm, however, from the one that I had experienced in New Mexico. This was a quiet, fleeting rhythm, with a definition and reality that defied the eye and penetrated within to become the vision of the pulse. Was this the spirit that Imam al-Ghazali refers to in his book, *The Jewels of the Quran,* that 'once seen opens the door of the unseen world?'[13] The spaces of my large canvases, though Euclidian in their crystalline dimensions, bore organic, undulating marks; repeated words of spiritual significance appeared as calligraphic gestures and color melted to become molten glass to reflect and suggest visions of a universal landscape, a landscape that did not dictate or echo anything tangible that was around me. I called these paintings Uniscapes, for these were visual manifestations of a cosmic-terrestrial space, united in time, and instrumental in leading me through the door to a new opening.

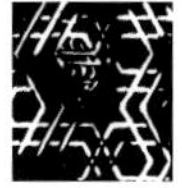

"It is not enough to recognize Truth
One must have the courage to act on it."
—Written in 2000

The Opening

I am now convinced that a work of art must have the potential to act as a conduit through which the spirit of the viewer is led into a dimensional plane in which time and space interface. In this space, the viewer is given the opportunity to swim in the recognition of her inner self. To impregnate this opportune moment, the artist has to step out of her body into a space-place where, like an alchemist, she turns paint, a dross material, into wondrous entities, capable of transporting the spirit of its viewer. In this state of being, the artist and the viewer both experience a brief glimpse of the soul of the universe, the artist while making the work, and the viewer in experiencing it. It is truly a moment out of time for it is a moment of suspension. It is a beautiful moment. In graduate school, I learnt that beauty in art is a moment of sublimity – the inexplicable aesthetic experience. Yet for me this beautiful moment is when I am touched by everything right as I move with the soul of the Universe. And they are rare moments in the art-making process for I can paint many paintings and not experience it. But it is a moment to wait for, as no other experience quite matches it. I think this momentous experience is like a sense of unity with all of my self. It is a state where the pools of consciousness are no longer limited to defined perception, and everything is on one single plane. This is my destiny, to think and move in paint, for it allows me to construct tangible visions through which I can reach an inexplicable state. I am convinced that this is what art philosophy is all about and what Wassily Kandinsky, the painter, was searching for and referred to as 'the music of the spheres.' Perhaps Imhotep, the architect, experienced a similar vision when he masterminded the stepped pyramid at Giza, or Myron, the sculptor, when he found the right gestural moment for the Discobolus, or the unknown architect who envisioned the Taj Mahal.

In *The Jewels of the Quran*, Imam al- Ghazali also talks about the alchemic transformation of a person's being when a person has acquired the 'capability of comprehending the hidden connection between the visible world and the invisible.'[13] He likens this experience to people who are in a perpetual state of sleep, awakening only at the time of this experience. He says that it is through reflection on similitude and imaginative symbols that one can get a glimpse of the spirit that lies latent within the sensuous. He argues that to be unmindful of the spirit in all things is similar to understanding the complexities of one's body but heedless to one's own spirit. Soyinke Wole, in her book *Myth, Literature and the African World* comes close to this idea when she refers to the artist as 'an intermediary quester transmitting knowledge of time that enhances human beings' existence with the cyclic consciousness of time.'

I see myself as an essence-quester seeking to inform myself of the hidden vitality that exists in the sensuous world. Although my visions are of an empirical nature, I am confronted, nonetheless, with the innate symmetries that lie latent within all complex natural phenomena. These, combined with my experiences, history, and feelings give rise to a vision polarized between cosmological ultimates – of genesis and extinction – and finalize into a magical metaphor of a more enlightened state of experience.

Consequently, I am driven to paint paintings where line, color, light, and texture, as animating forces, form visual propositions that invite the viewer to take a salmon-like leap of faith into an unknown realm. Similar to Ludwig Wittgenstein, I too have come to believe that "human understanding will never penetrate or surpass the absolute. The meaning of the world, as I understand it, must lie outside the world and cannot be understood and comprehended by [images] logic or intelligible speech such as ethics, eternity or God."[14] Hence my paintings are to be seen for what they are and what they are not in order to make an assessment of what is true and what is not true. It is good that each person who views my paintings comes with a set of queries, for no response is a virgin one. It is these questions that decide the truth of what it is that they are seeing. At that moment, the painting can become true or false, depending on the depth of the viewer; thus the viewer changes the nature of what the painting is.

Vortex Existence

Along with gifted moments, I go through what I call vortex existences. These are periods when I cannot really express anything in paint. My mind is unable to transform my feelings into image-forms, necessary to start the visual creative process. Experiences have an emotive nature, and these in turn, if meaningful, are sustained through feelings and conjured as image-forms, which we all envision in the various dimensional sub-stations of our mind. These image-forms are not concretions but mind-creations remaining in a fluxing, atom-energy state, and are perhaps experienced by most individuals. A visual artist differs from others when she feels compelled to make these mind-creations tangible in visual manifestations of light, color, texture, and form.

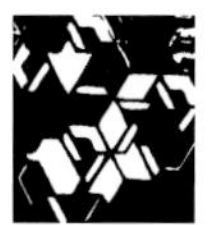

Once you see the vision
you've got to follow it to the end,
even if no one shows up to cheer and
you wind up speaking to the wind.[15]

— Rabi'a al-Adawiyya

The Artist's Vision

Each individual is born with an inner language that is uniquely personal. It comes out of a vision that they experience, cultivated by the way they live their life. Rabi'a, the twelfth century poet, was not far off when she said, "your life is the only opportunity that life can give you, if you ignore it, if you waste it, all that will remain of you is dust." So perhaps all that I have written is a conversation to myself, with myself, and maybe with all my fellow artists. It is 'art talk.' Conversations like these may help us move from the language of words into the language of visuals, and to enter a realm similar to that of *Suleiman* (Solomon) *(-AAS)* the prophet. We don't have *Suleiman's (-AAS)* hoopoe bird to reveal the secrets of the non-human kingdoms, so we have to rely on ourselves to penetrate the kingdom of shape-forms.

Unity of forms

Where pools of consciousness are no longer defined perception
And the lines of the unknown weave definite patterns.
Here the void churns, turns, and becomes fathomable;
Valleys fade, and all nature transcends — I am stilled.
The primordial, the waters, the sphere, all are parts of tomorrow —
of an older past; Here everything praises the circle.
Colors lay and overlay, heralding a new, age-old universality.
And I move from the limitations of cognition,
of past, present, and future.

— Written in 1984

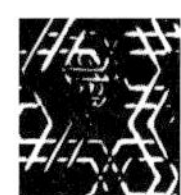

Something stirred within but yet I did not know how to enter the world of my inner vision. I could see it in my head but could not manifest it in paint.
I just did not have the tools. So I painted not so much concerned with what I was achieving but enjoying the act of simply painting. I was conversing with nature. It was an art conversation.

— page 34

An Art Conversation

As an essence-quester, the search begins with my own self, realizing the impact of what I have inherited from the first human, the legendary Adam, and the timeless ride that I am on. So I start this conversation with an ode to Adam vis-à-vis to myself.

Ode to the First Human
Adam unveiled,
Out of perfection, of proportion and balance
Lost in the confines of mortality.
Taking form but formless,
Constantly changing, physically transforming,
Forever constant.
Estranged from the Beloved,
Beguiled by reflections,
Lost in the unreal but ever so close to the Real.

— Written in 2006 after completing painting of Adam

I believe that a painter's search for self realization is most original when she aspires for forms of expression wrought out of her knowledge of what she understands as true, her experience of the painting process as a continuum, and her desire for excelling in the process of painting. At this point, she is not given to any form of hype, commercialism, ambition, or play. Rather, she is driven into a state of intense introspection to find something personally profound that reveals the reason for her existence. Andre Malraux calls such people (painters) "outcasts" for their paintings are "subordinate to nothing outside of itself," furnished by a burning desire to understand their existence through life experiences, and guided only by their intuitive senses and an inherited criterion. A painting then is simply an expressive system of paint markings that shapes what the painter is revealing about herself at that time, place, and space in the context of a revelation.

The Painted Mark

In paintings, a painted mark is the path of a moving point of energy and a visible action. When we paint with marks, we make musical gestures and, like everything that has to do with music, there is vibration, hence a sustained energy field. Each painted mark through its vibration is uniquely alive, radiating an energy field which in turn sustains the next mark. Each painting, then, is a system of expressed order within which the forms are organized through *their* own structural and dynamic considerations.

When I am painting with marks of energy, I am dealing with the plurality of perceptual moments. Each mark becomes a perceptual encounter, as perception is happening all the time. The painting is a result of what is left behind as a result of these encounters. Thus the painting is the totality of the many processes of my conceptual and visual development.

In the painting of these moments I bring the mind's eye to collaborate with the imagination, memory, and visual sensation. I do this by letting the physical eyes become the window to the different parts of my brain.

My working method is that of a 'scientist.' Using *dhikr* – the remembrance faculty – to provide suggestive imagery, I draw forms that are wrought out from the materials of paint and unbridle their expressive potentials. As I paint, I formulate my thoughts, my intent, and my needs, and from this exchange the struggle begins between what it is that I want to say and what the material wants to do. It is not a struggle for domination as it is only I that feel the tension. Rather it is a struggle on my part to fuse together the materials that I use with the forms of my thought. There is an anxious vulnerability from which I seek tranquility. By constantly blending, transforming, and remaking the surface of the picture plane and by exploring layers of contextual meaning, I hope to rekindle a sense of wonder and wholeness in the contemporary heart.

The 'remembrance faculty' is an induced memory-state of mind where I take selected signs and interface them to an inner vision. Used as a method, it becomes a conscious Way that leads me to draw on events, situations, and objects from the realm of the sensory, the imaginal, and the suprasensory. It is a tool by which I can come to understand a particular moment in time and space, not as an object or event but as an action that is *alive* to the cross-currents of change and experimentation, yet fertilized by the collective perception, regardless of boundaries or borders. In this way, the *experience – field* always remains activated.

Words, letters, and symbols come from my immediate consciousness to charge the meaning and purpose of the images. These are applied in an unobtrusive way but with a mission to register at some level within the viewer's consciousness. There is never any attempt at atmosphere, shadow, perspective, or modeling. Each mark of color remains independent yet perceptibly connected to the galaxical energy surrounding it. My goal is to make an alchemic transformation of color-forms into particles of 'energy as light' that lie hidden in us and around us. In this way I try by 'insight' to find the archetypal nature-forms around us.

It is said that 'Reason itself is its own reason' and that built into it is the remembrance faculty that reminds reason that all things return to oneness. This oneness can be comprehended by the processes of self-disclosure and of vision, which in turn may lift the veils of the natural worlds in order to penetrate the realm of the inexplicable and concealed. Perhaps, in this way, I join artists such as Wassily Kandinsky, Arthur Dove, and Barnett Newman, for whom the purpose of painting was to allow us to see the unseeable "and to lift the veils of the incomprehensible reality."

There is always something forming from the unformed and it is this 'formed' that is perceived as an object or thing by the human mind. For the painter the canvas takes on the architecture of the local mind within which possible clues and explanations are sought. The brush is the 'mouse,' that the hand moves to access the 'folders' of the psycho-physical cerebral centers, all the time questioning the visual impressions that appear through 'the window' of the physical eye. For the expressive painter the painting is a reminder that the visual world as we see it is very much a construction of our contextual development. This development is based on the painter's own intellectual, psychological, cultural, and educational growth. The painted world is a unique, contextual world, deriving its forms from the natural and cognitive world that each person resides in. Each painted mark made in *that* context becomes an expression of spiritual insight. Thus when we are painting, we are like the bloodhound following the *scent* of the momentary encounter, acting on suggestions, listening, interpreting, inferring, and relying on our intuition. In this way, we go beyond the 'I' and all the various perceptual stations to reach an insight regarding our subject matter that surpasses all optical foundations and humanization of objects, and overcomes dullness as well as slavery to measures of photography and technique.

There is that question of reality that seems to plague some of us. I, for one, refuse certain realities – realities that I consider artificial, needs that are not essential but fabricated. Most of these needs are the result of media, for the world of Advertisement not only interferes with our imagination but also dulls our color sense and our innate perception. It is not without reason that, in 1966, professor and activist Mario Savio wisely stated:

> "There's a time when the operation of the machine becomes so odious, makes you so sick at heart, that you can't take part, you can't even passively take part, and you've got to put your bodies upon the gears and upon the wheels, upon the levers, upon all the apparatus, and you've got to make it stop! And you've got to indicate to the people who run it, to the people who own it, that unless you're free, the machine will be prevented from working at all!"

Taking Savio's thoughts to heart, and staying ahead of his forecasted time and freeing myself from the constant bombardment of the world of television and media, I as a painter, consciously and unconsciously, seek another color, another form, an elusive color form that is deep and capable of expressing intrinsic and essential values and independent of the virtual world of

Advertisement. A glimpse into reality is by rediscovering essential values, and the painting process allows me to do just that by exploring the shifting, textural, life-giving, color-sound-forms present in our world that are untainted, unsegregated, and non-denatured by the commercial world. Reality, as I comprehend, is obtained not by limiting myself to one or two senses, but by exploring and correlating *all* my senses in order to produce the 'significant sense' of my visual world.

Painting Process and its Objective

Like the artist-teacher Robert Henri, I too believe:

> "The object of a painting is not to make a picture (Art)… however unreasonable this may sound; the picture is merely a by-product and may be useful, valuable and interesting as a sign of what has passed. The object behind every fine work of art is the attainment of a state of being, a state of high functioning, and a more than ordinary moment of existence. In such moments activity is inevitable, its result is but a trace, a byproduct of that state, a footprint. … they are of interest (value) to others, because they are to some extent (at least) readable and reveal the possibilities of a greater existence."

This attitude on the part of the painter requires that the painter maintain her position in society as an independent thinker and a non-integrated individual. She must, in a way, 'sink in solitude' and cultivate a form of seclusion for herself in order to be serious, original and preserve her innate integrity. Yet at the same time she cannot turn her back on all that is negative around her, which includes an open, indulgent, demoralized art environment driven to a great extent by electronic media and greed. By pursuing her own path, regardless of all these persuasions, she makes a contribution by simply being the antidote for an afflicted society.

Yet it is paint through which a painter speaks. Each painting is a work of art in which a composition of pigment and binder known as paint is used as a medium of expression, in order to endow a surface with quasi-magical and transportable qualities. It is through the process of grinding, mixing, and pouring dense substance such as pigment, solvents, binders, and emulsions that preconception loses itself within the chaos of forming and in dying gives rise to a new understanding of existence manifested in a visual form for that time. Thus each painting unfolds as an object-concept presenting the viewer with the possibility that the inherent forms of life can be penetrated and visualized. This painting process allows the artist to take a centripetal approach back into the object's *batin* or esoteric form, for what we see in nature is the object's conclusive, centrifugal manifestation of energy-burst: the *zahir* of form, its exoteric character.

When painting with this objective in mind, each object in horizontal (chronological and physical time) – *zaman afaqi* – can be led back into its inner region, which corresponds to it in polar, or vertical (spatial-Para conscious time) – *zaman afros*. This process of visualization may be achieved through a state of contemplation/reflection where resonance and reverberation interface. In this state of mind, one recognizes universal, structural components that give life to objects but lie outside the everyday temporal frame. By learning to internalize and be attentive to these regions, the artist is rewarded further in having the ability to perceive the zones of paranormal colored lights by which these objects are spirited and structured. Through the practices of *dhikr* (penetrative remembrances of being), our visionary apperception may be inspired to connect Noumena (as opposed to the limitations of phenomenon) with the physiology of suprasensory centers or zones (*kiswar*) in our 'resurged body.' Could the act of painting utilize similar practices and act as a conduit to direct us, step-by-step, inward toward the vertical pole, the place of the ontological axis?

On Color

The surface of a canvas is an existential ground where the artist's pattern of consciousness may be traced through the markings. Hence the surface symbolizes the artist's state of being as well as the artist's state of consciousness for *that* period of time. There is a natural tendency for color planes to delimit shape and determine a particular character. When painting, ask the question, what is the character of this shape? What does it wish to be? Then, think of the color.

Form happens when you add the color. Form is the character of the shape. Everything has color. You just have to have the eyes to see it. We lose our sight in total light and total darkness. Both instances share similar seeing qualities and yet in each case there is a different sense and feeling of sight. Black can appear cold and unyielding and its opacity may weigh heavily on the mind; thus we may seek to lighten the heaviness by varying tonalities of color. However, we can also think of black as compression of all color and enrich its opaque surface with color transparencies of a textural nature to produce openings that absorb light, and in turn cast dimensional shadows. Translucent color communicates an estranged and implacable feeling of dimensional richness.

On Design

Design is a concept and an abstraction.
Conceptualize through design; but in the art making process forget it.
Now, think in terms of rhythm, for rhythm is reality.
Rhythm is the pulse and at the same time the space between two pulse beats.
It sounds the music within us and connects us with its similitude.
In a work of art, rhythm grows out of its own coherently expressed structure.

On Space

Think of Space as aqueous,
permeating into every crack, corner, and crevice,
including the space occupied by energy-form.
Every object, to exist, must push its way out
by agitating and changing the dynamics
on and in the surface and volume of space.
Each entity is a formed drop within the waters of space.

On Universal Archetypes

> Serious Art must simply not be based on phantasms, sexual obsessions, and the chance happenings of daily life, i.e. *true art transcends surface turbulence.*
>
> — Alberto Giacometti 1935

Like Giacometti, I too agonize over the issue of transience and anecdote. Giacometti realized that "in all human beings there is a deep and unchanging core which is only slightly modified by differences in time, place and culture."[16] It was important for him to discover this core within himself and transfer this knowledge into his art. I understand the core to be the fundamental essence that speaks to a universality that rises above all boundaries of race, geography, culture, and mentality and formalizes as an archetype that communicates to all human beings. The archetype has absorbed a likeness that reflects a 'presence' whereby when we find it and gaze at it, it awakens in us a feeling about the irreconcilable elements that coexist, like the concurrence of life and death, joy and grief, wonder and disbelief. In its presence we are imbued with a deeper understanding of reality.

My understanding of universal archetypes on the other hand is that they are the unchanging options of the Divine and may be understood as similitudes.[17] In the world of Traditional Knowledge, the world of similitude is a place where higher planes of existence are reflected as forms and that the world of the imagination may interface with the world of similitudes. Some Traditionalists believe that at a certain spiritual level, the doors to a sensory universe – *mundus imaginalis* – is opened and here one experiences "a concrete spiritual world of archetype-figures."[18] Suhrawardi, the twelth century Muslim philosopher, affirms this 'sensory universe' as "having its own contour, dimension and extension in space and not to be compared with the shape and spatiality as we perceive them in the world of physical bodies."[19] It is possible that under the right conditions, the right intentions and with Heart, an individual can enter this realm to find forms that correspondence to Divine qualities?

Traditional cultures both of the east and the west have seen the sphere and its counterpart the circle to be endowed with cosmic laws of proportions and symmetry and thus equivalent of eternity and unity. Even Plato, influenced by Pythagorean thought, considered the sphere the most perfect of solids containing within itself the five regular polygons to which Al Baruni related the elements: earth – cube, hexahedron – bounded by six squares, water – icosahedron – consisting of twelve equilateral triangles, air – octahedron – eight equilateral triangles, fire – tetrahedron – four equilateral triangles, and the universe itself as the sphere – dodecahedron made up of twelve pentagons.[20] Perhaps Al Baruni's thesis was based on the fact that certain geometrical shapes with their corresponding forms from nature were used through the ages for their ability to penetrate deep into our unconsciousness to stir feelings and remembrances within our collective mind. It is not a coincidence that forms that are spherical and circular in nature have a special significance to us humans. Take for example, the sun, the moon and the human eye; both occidental and oriental cultures have given them powerful attributes of the Divine. Perhaps it is because the perfect sphere resides within us in the form of the human eye, the organ through which we can reflect the bounties of nature and find the answer to our existence through our Intellect and our own Perfect Nature.

The Man of Light or the Enlightened One has been known by many names in various cultures. Suhrawardi speaks of the Enlightened One as the Perfect Nature that is within all human beings. I remember my father narrating a wonderful anecdote from Suhrawardi's *Kitab al-Istamakhis,* on Perfect Nature. It was an advice Aristotle gave to his pupil, Alexander of Macedonia. Interestingly enough, I was to find the entire quote in Henry Corbin's *The Man of Light*:

Wise Socrates declared that Perfect Nature is called the sun of the philosopher, the original *root* of his being and at the same time the *branch* springing from him. Hermes was asked: "How does one achieve knowledge or wisdom? How can one bring it down to his world below?" Through Perfect Nature," he answered. "What is the root of wisdom?" "Perfect Nature." "What is the key to Wisdom?" "Perfect Nature." "What then is Perfect Nature?" he was asked. "It is the heavenly entity, the philosopher's Angel, conjoined with his star, which rules him and opens the doors of wisdom for him, teaches him what is difficult, reveals to him what is right, in sleeping and in waking.[21]

Universal archetypes, like all other archetypes, take form in our mind but are free from its control; they are born in the hold of gravity yet not subject to its laws. They are derived from our perception of natural phenomena but soar out of it, defying time and enduring through change, synthesis, and transformation. They take form when humans look at the world and see Divinity reflected. Are they relevant in an age that seems to be obsessed with fantasy, narcissism, superficiality, transience, and the artifice? Perhaps for these very reasons they are.

Universal archetypes are a means to express "all of life" in a form that is of a collective nature, connected to its Source yet autonomous, with a renewed sense of power, beauty, and mystery. These forms exist because of the significance of their *functional iconography* and have perhaps been transmitted to us through dreams from our collective unconscious mind or from heredity, as Jung would have us believe, or perhaps, at that moment, we were touched by the Breath of the Divine.

On Knowledge

I have often wondered why some of us have an innate urgency to acquire knowledge. Ali ibn Abi Talib (RA), one of the four rightly guided *Khalifa* – civil and religious rulers – of early Islam and prophet Mohammed's *(-AAS)* first cousin, equated Knowledge to Truth, and provided a method through which it could be acquired. He set up a premise in which he defined knowledge as enlightenment but at the same time defined it as an evolving process. He set up the station of empiricism by stressing the role of the intellect to reason the material assessed. He expanded the consciousness of the mind to acknowledge the role of intuition as a guiding factor in research and experimentation and that truth as knowledge and vice versa could only be attained if The Creator of all creation allowed the truth to be revealed. In the end, all knowledge is acquired, *Inshallah* – if the Creator wishes. The religious scholar Jafer as Sadiq (RA) expounded the ideas of Ali ibn Abi Talib on knowledge and defined it as "Enlightenment of the heart is its essence, Truth is its principal object, Inspiration is its guide, Reason is its acceptor, God is its Inspirer, and the word of man are its utterers."[22]

Our curiosity is aroused as we live in our environments. We question, investigate, speculate, and conclude. Acceptance and the desire to accommodate and conform are the most normal way to exist with our fellow human beings. However, there are those who question further and dig deeper into phenomena that are of a more complex and sometimes esoteric in the physical and spiritual world.

Knowledge implies a search to recognize, identify, acquire, and structure information from a given place of origin. Knowledge is the way to expand the impregnated '*spatial place*' in which our being resides. But it is only when we give meaning to that 'place' that knowledge begins to have a conceptual face, taking shape and form. However, the conceptual form is not the final form for a painter as she has to turn the mental idea into a painted entity. It is at this stage that the painter is entirely in the hands of the Source-Giver, inspiration, and intuition. When all three players drive the painter's hands, she creates forms that are 'spiritual projections,' comprehended by an inner sight that goes beyond sensory and perceptual experience.

Hence knowledge is the way we reaffirm and regenerate our insight and intuitive capabilities. A painter uses the art processes to convert knowledge into comprehensible forms. If this conversion is done correctly, there is an alchemic transformation of the unseen into the seen. A "spatial place" begins to take shape where forms begin to unravel the previously known answers to existential life. These are "wisdom-forms," portals to our many levels of consciousness that enable us to see the world through wondrous lens.

Outside the tunnel in the Open

> It is the artist's job to imagine the most impossible things. These are not answers. They are just possible entries into hidden things.
>
> — Anselm Keifer

My life as a painter has made me acknowledge an age-old tradition which states that prior to our human birth we reside in our being – our soul. I understand it to be a spatial place of a pre-verbal nature where all forms of communication are through tele-cognizance, and in the form of Noumenal images through senses beyond our perception. I have come to understand that the 'heart'—the center of our feelings—is really the spirit acting through the body yet independent of it. The spirit, the active reflection of the soul, is energized by and acts through the portals of our senses to make our body perform conscious actions. I have also come to understand that the materials with which I make my paintings are similar to my body parts, shaped by the spirit of my mind. As I make every effort to perfect my craft to give form to my vision, I come closer to realizing that the painted object of this endeavor is just a shadow of the changing reflection that burns within, even though each painting for that moment appears to have captured a glimpse of that vision. The finality of each vision remains in a contained, obscure, spiral space, teasing me to manifest it, if I can. As a painter, my challenge is to ride on the back of horizontal and vertical time, rocking between centrifugal and centripetal zones as they fold and enfold to reach a place where the painted space reflects unity of being. Each painting, through changing forms, becomes a painted trace of that glimpse into the preverbal realm. This kind of immersion can be likened to worship because the ultimate aim is not impression, expression, or narration; rather the painting is simply a Way to touch the spirit of the soul.

Endnotes

1 The Bengal Presidency included the provinces of West and East Bengal, Orissa, Assam, and Uttar Pradesh.

2 See Jyotsna Singh's excellent assessment on the meaning of the word *Nawob* (Nawab) that was given by the British to the indigenous people during the colonization of India, in her book: *Colonial Narratives.*

3 *Quran*. Chapter 7, verse 11-17: "Give me respite till the day they are raised up"…. 17: "Then will I assault them from before them and behind them, from their right and their left…"

4 *Wudu*: Prescribed method of cleansing yourself with water before going into the act of *salat* (Arabic) or *namaz* as it is called in Farsi, Urdu, or Bengali. The act entails preparation for the readiness of the mind and heart while going through the various acts of washing the hands, face and parts of the face, head, arms, and feet.

5 *Salat*: Prescribed method of worshipping Allah (See endnote 1). This method of worship is performed five times a day and was taught to the Muslims by Prophet Mohammed (SWM.) who in turn was taught by the Angel Gabriel. Every Muslim performs salat in the same manner. With the exception of the Arab world, worship is generally referred to as *namaz*, a Farsi term.

6 The year Prophet Mohammed emigrated from Makkah to Medina is known as the first year of the Muslim calendar. The emigration took place in 622 CE.

7 Trinh T. Minh-ha. *Women Native Other* (Indiana University Press, 1989), p.107.

8 *Quran*

9 Coelho, Paul, *The Alchemist* (Harper Collins Publishers, 1988), p. 22.

10 Also *Zuhr*: "afternoon" in Arabic.

11 Paul Coelho, in *The Alchemist,* refers to these as "mysterious forces."

12 In classical Indian music, melodies are divided according to their gender. *Ragni* are female melodies.

13 Al-Ghazali, *Jewels of the Quran* (Kegan Paul International United, 1983), p. 51.

14 Bruce Dufy, *The World as I Found it* (Ticknor and Fields, 1987).

15 Charles Upton, *Door Keeper of the Heart: Versions of Rabi'a* (Threshold Books, 1988), p. 49.

16 Charles Juliet, *Giacometti* (Universe Books, 1986), p. 49.

17 Naser Ardalan and Laleh Bakhtiar, *The Sense of Unity* (University of Chicago Press, 1973), p.

18 Henry Corbin, *The Man of Light* (Omega Publications, 1994), p. 42.

19 Corbin, *The Man of Light*, p. 43.

20 Renee Guénon, *Reign of Quantity*. From the chapter on qualified Space.

21 Corbin, *The Man of Light*, p. 17.

22 Translated by Sayed Ali Reza. "Peak of Eloquence" *NAHJUL BALAGHA: Takrike* (Tarsile Qu'ran, Inc., 1996), p. 70.

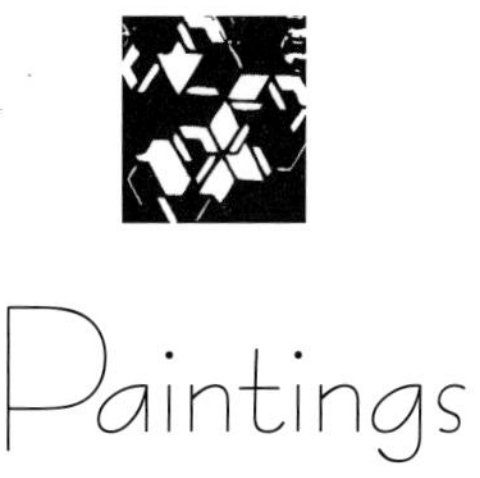

Paintings

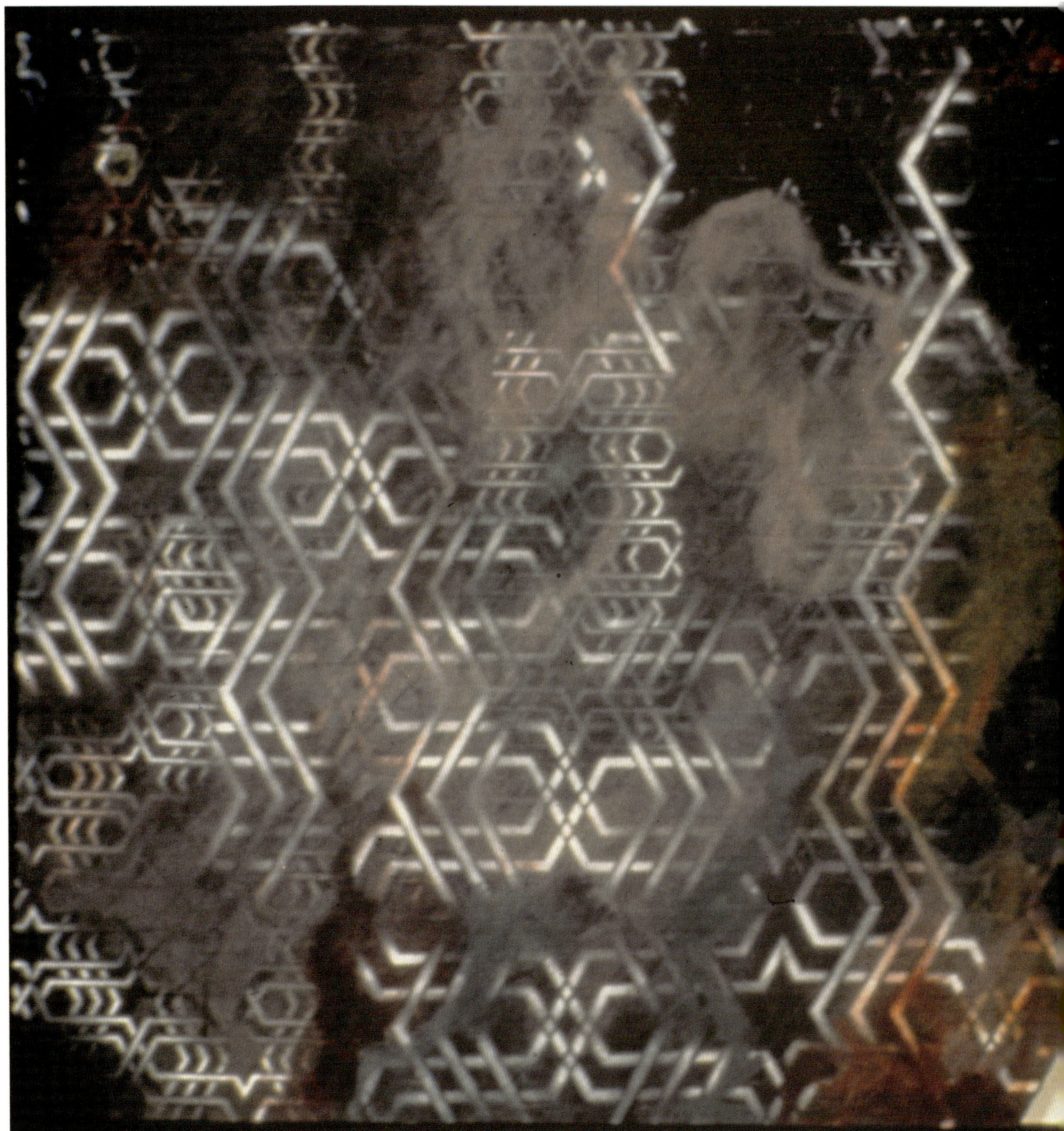

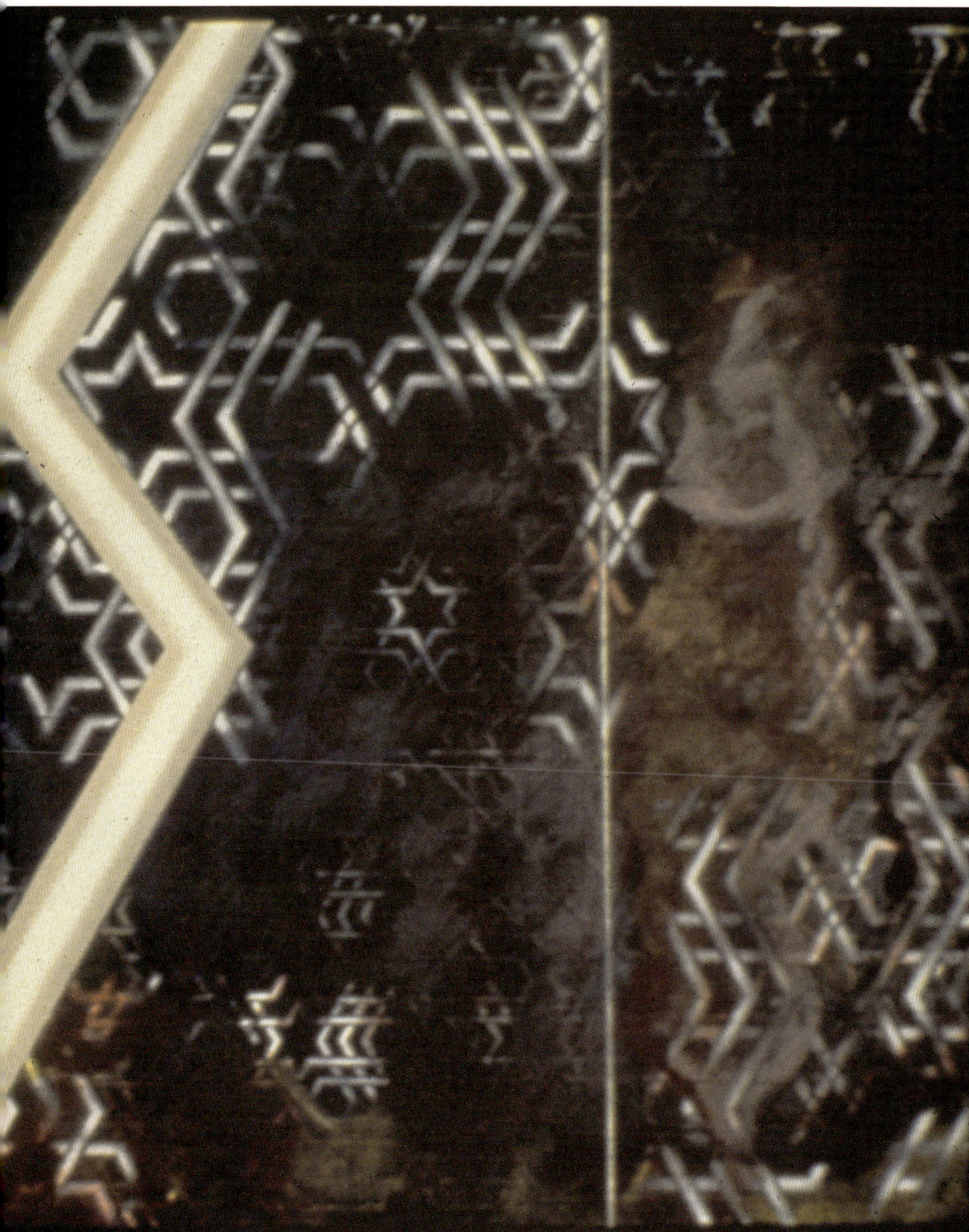

The Straight Path — *Sirat al Mustaquim*

1992

Oil/rubber on canvas

60" x 120"

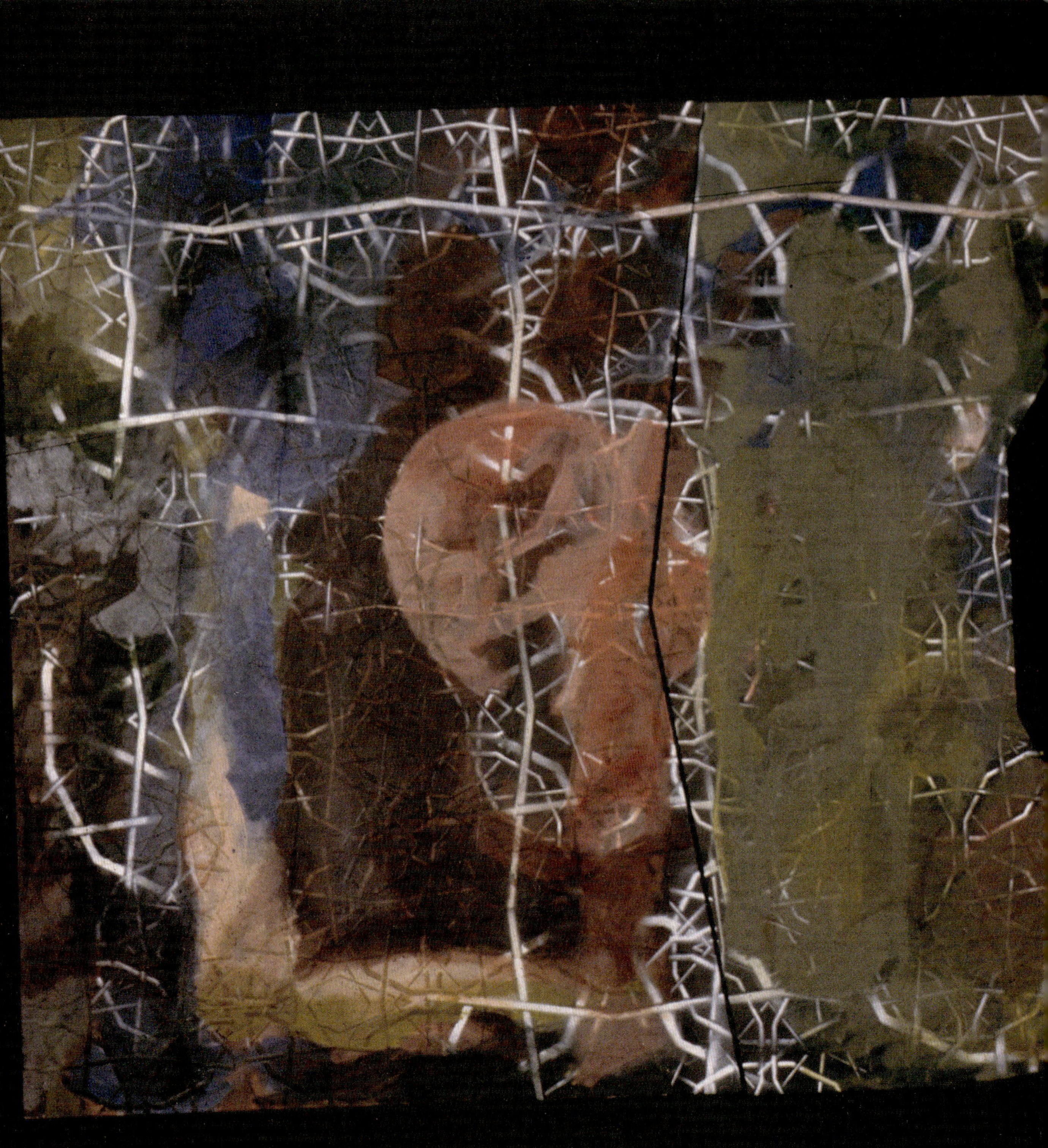

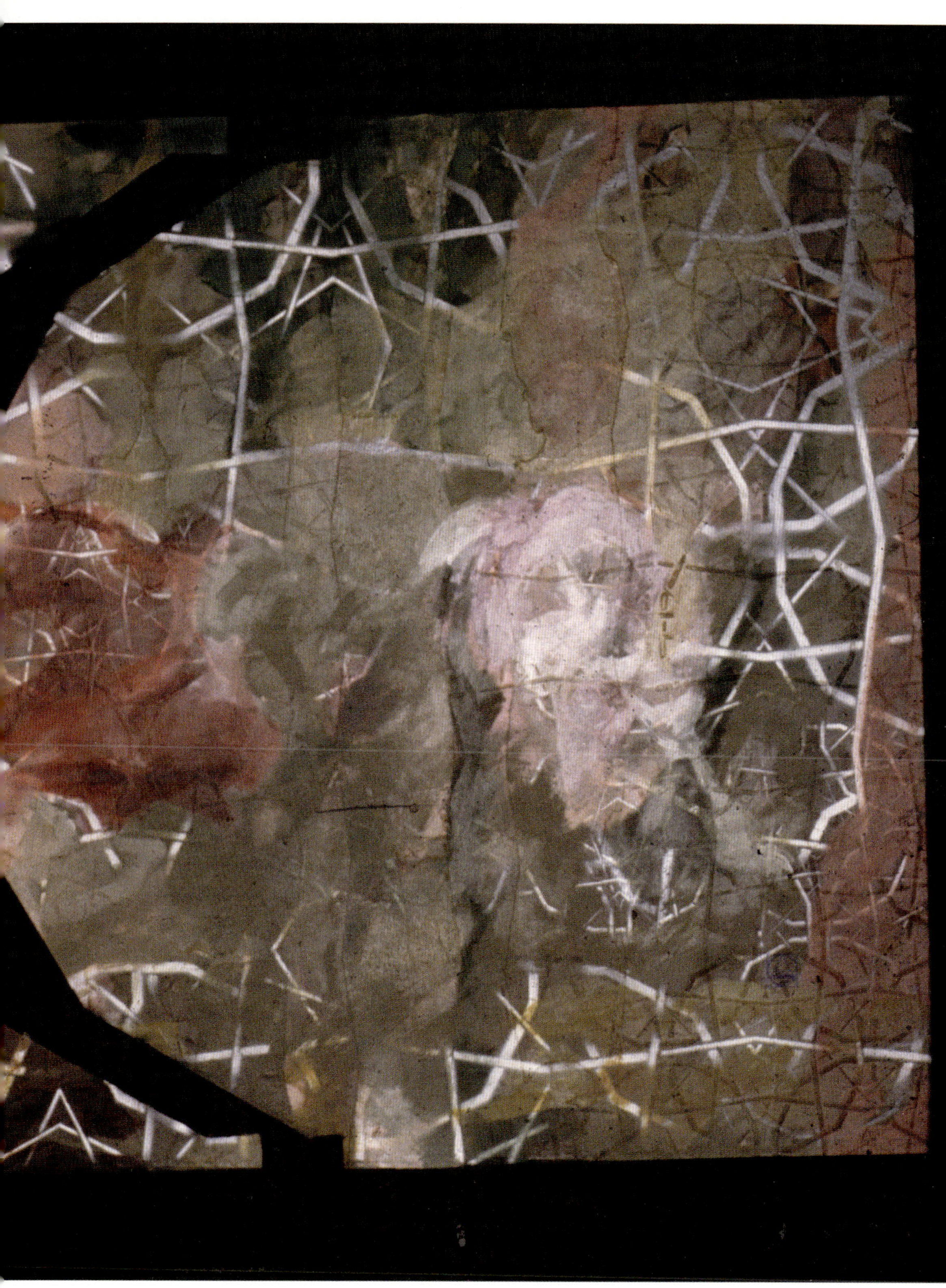

The Remaking

1992
Oil/Rubber
on Canvas
60" x 120"

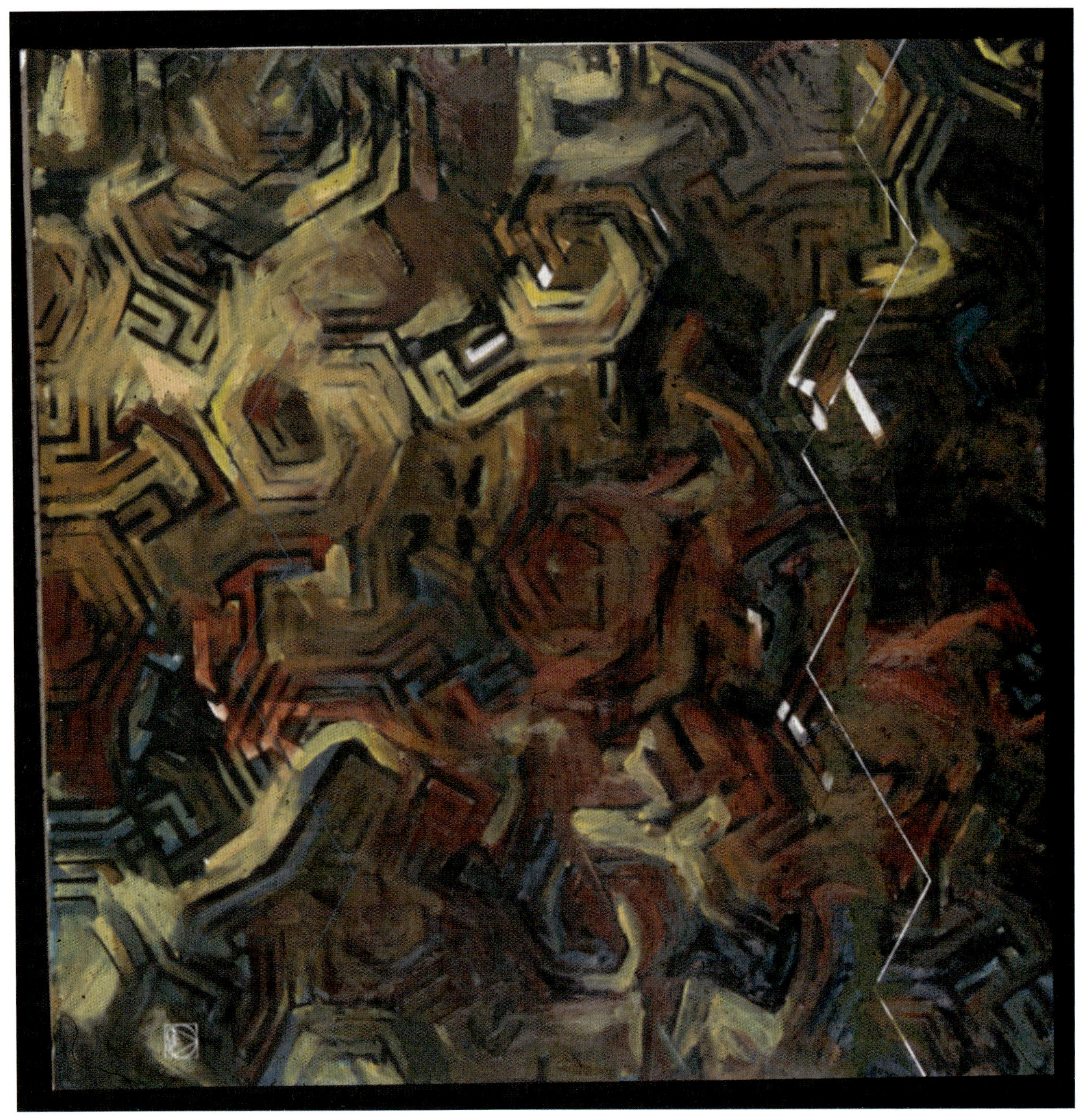

The Line of the Nabi(s). 1993. Oil/Rubber on Canvas. 60" by 60".

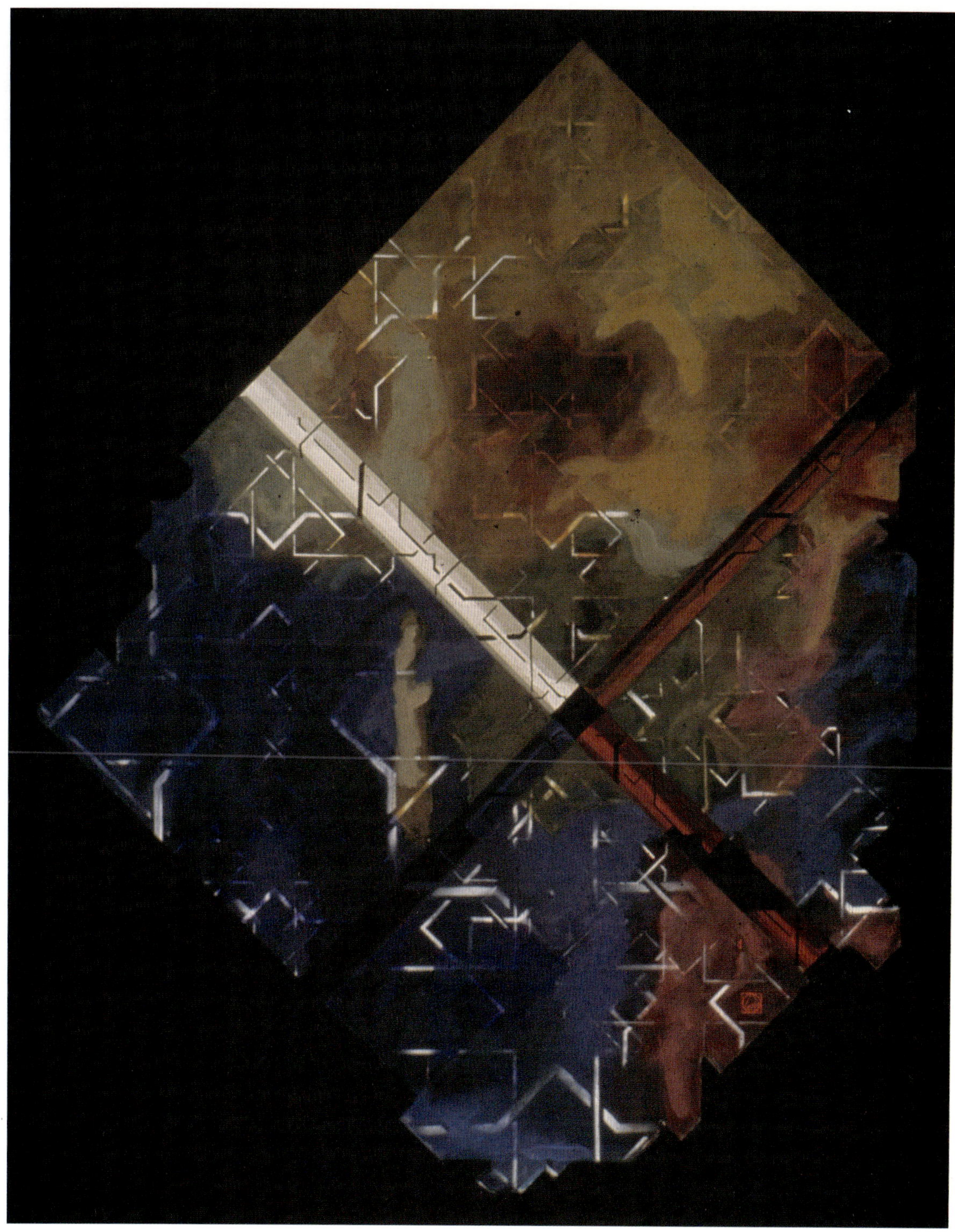

The
Square
in the
Garden of
Four
Rivers

1992
Oil on Canvas
and Wood
54" by 46"

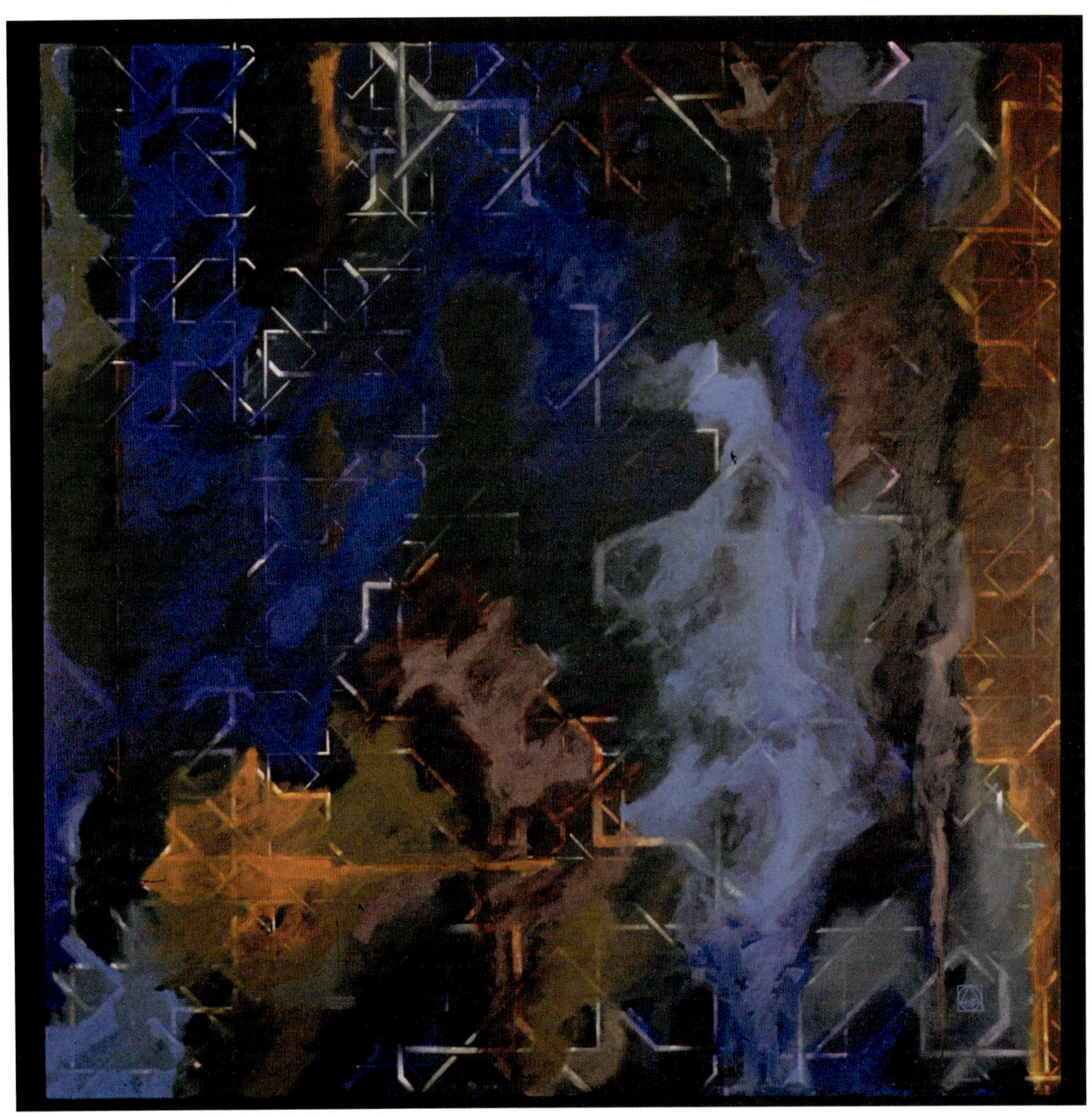

The Spring. 1991. Oil on Canvas. 60" by 60".

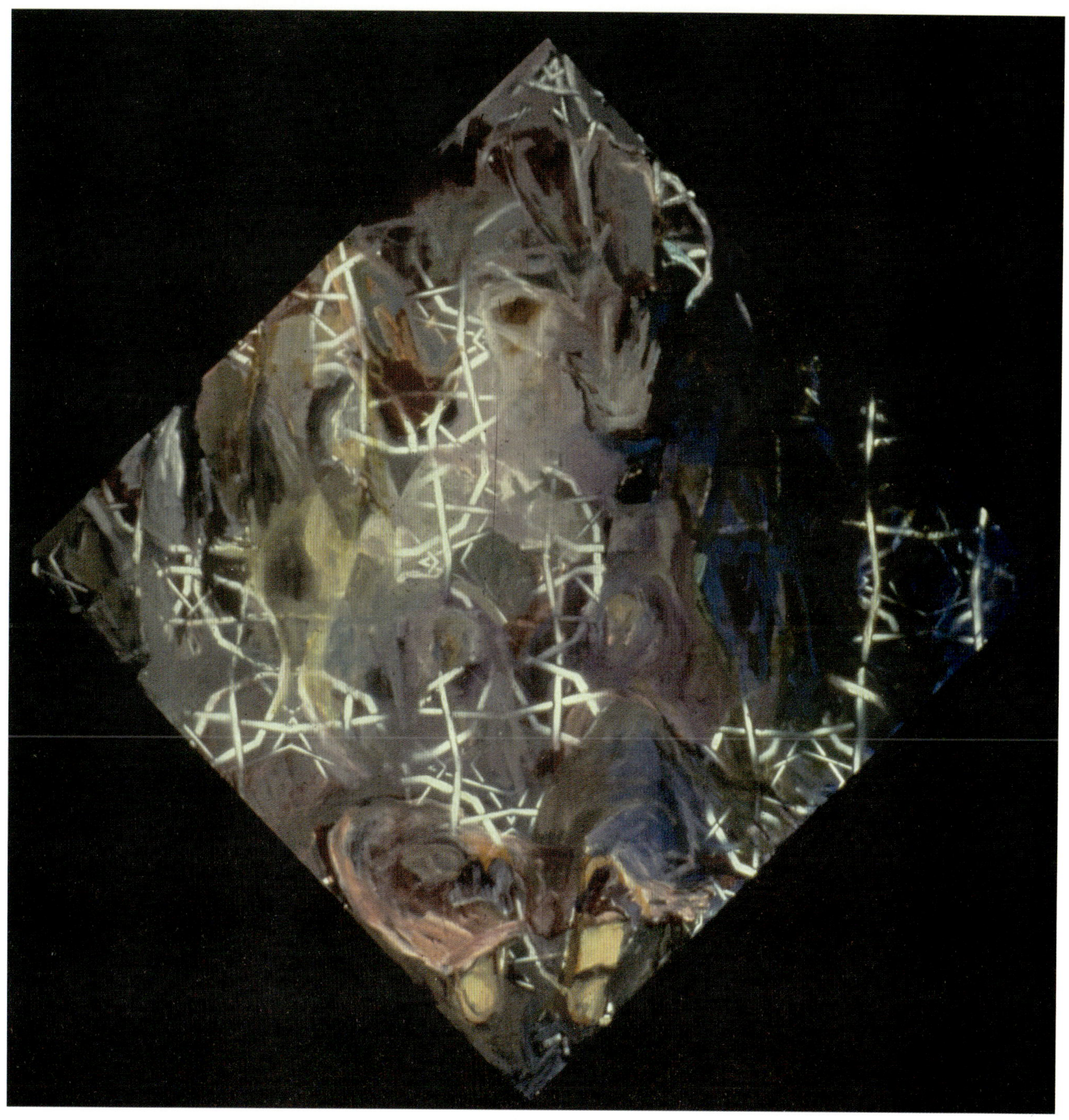

The Adoration No. 1. 2000. Oil/Mixed Media on Canvas. 42" by 42".

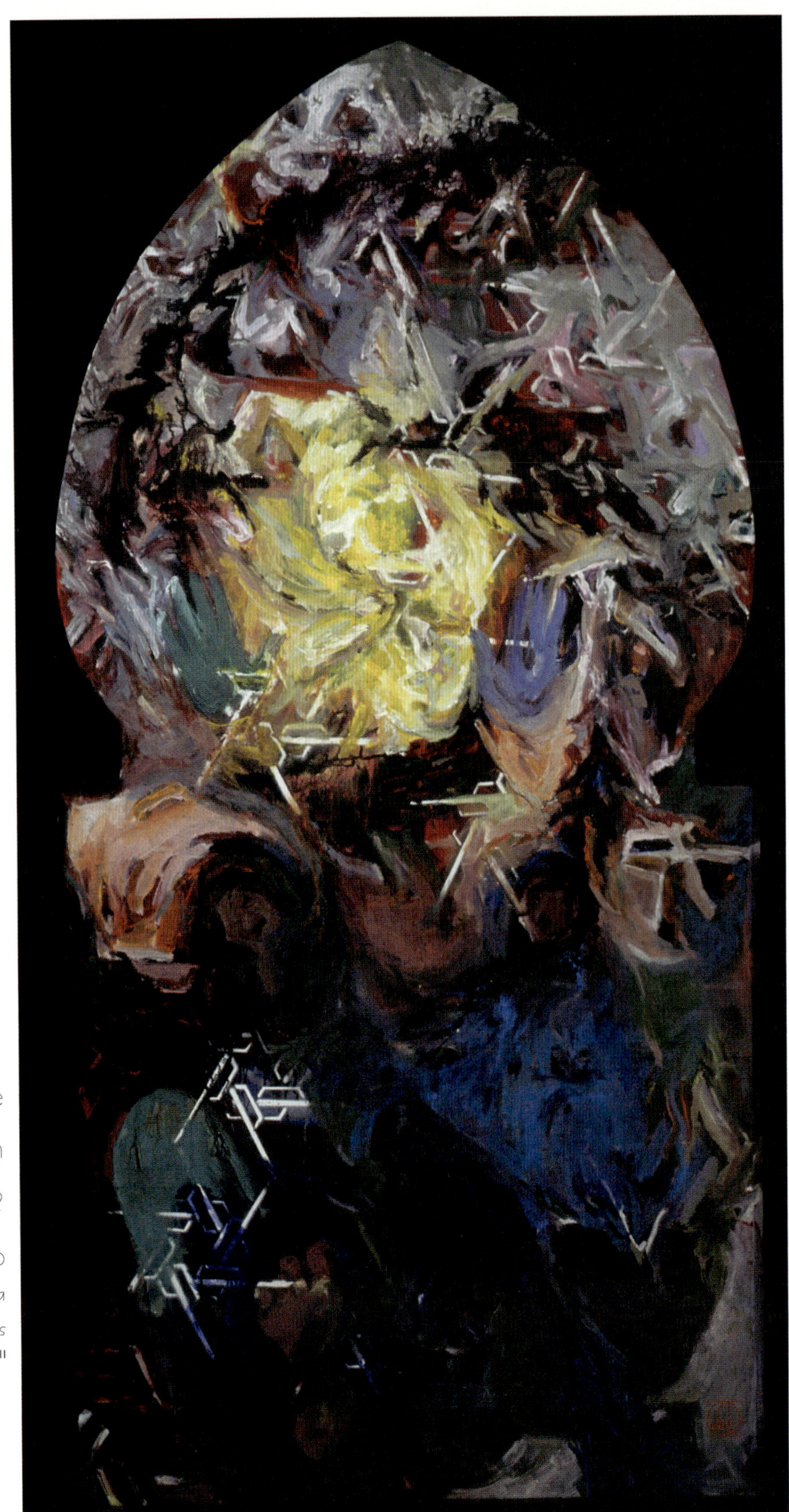

The Adoration No. 2

2000
Oil/Mixed Media on Canvas
60" by 30"

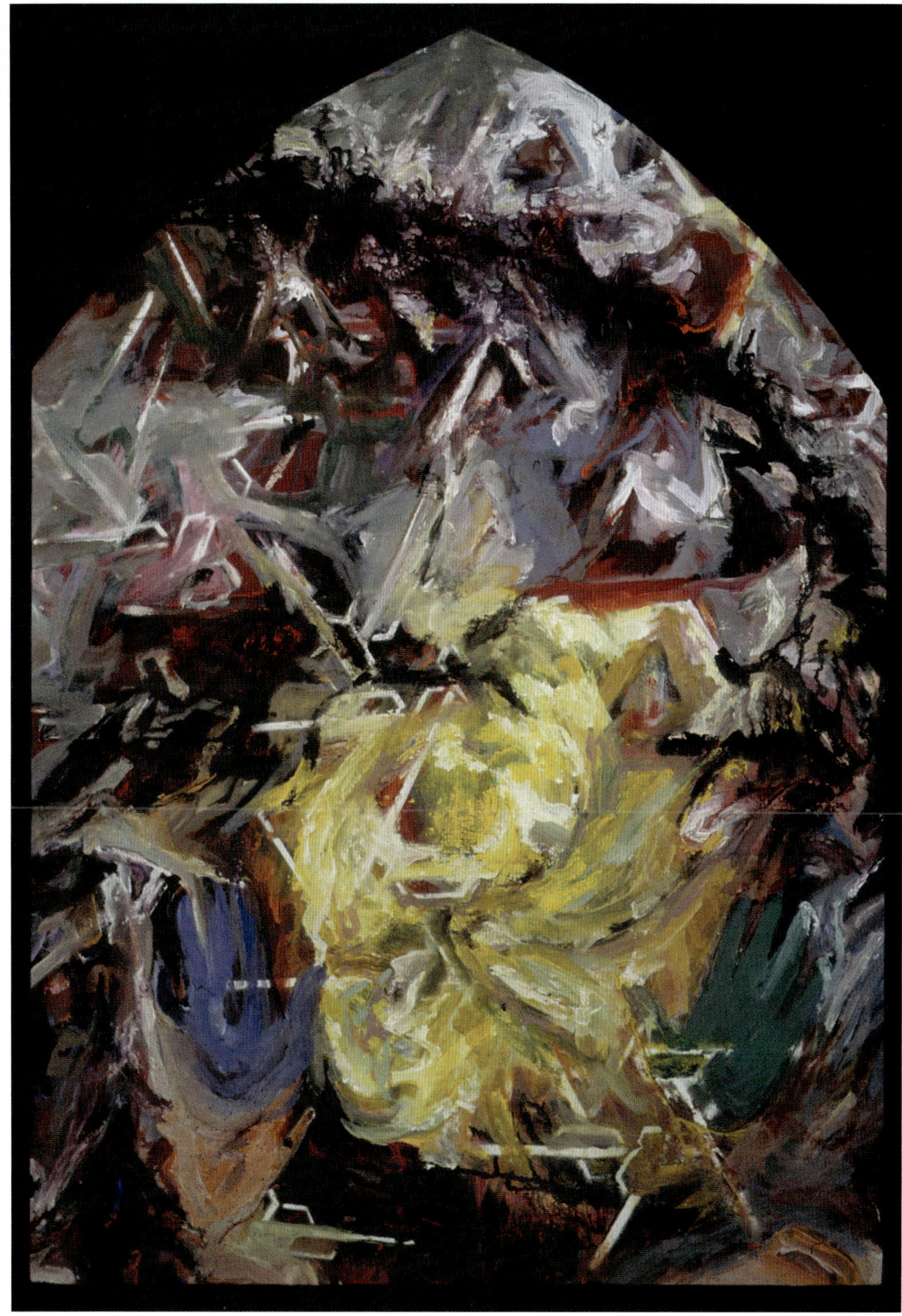

Detail of "The Adoration No. 2"

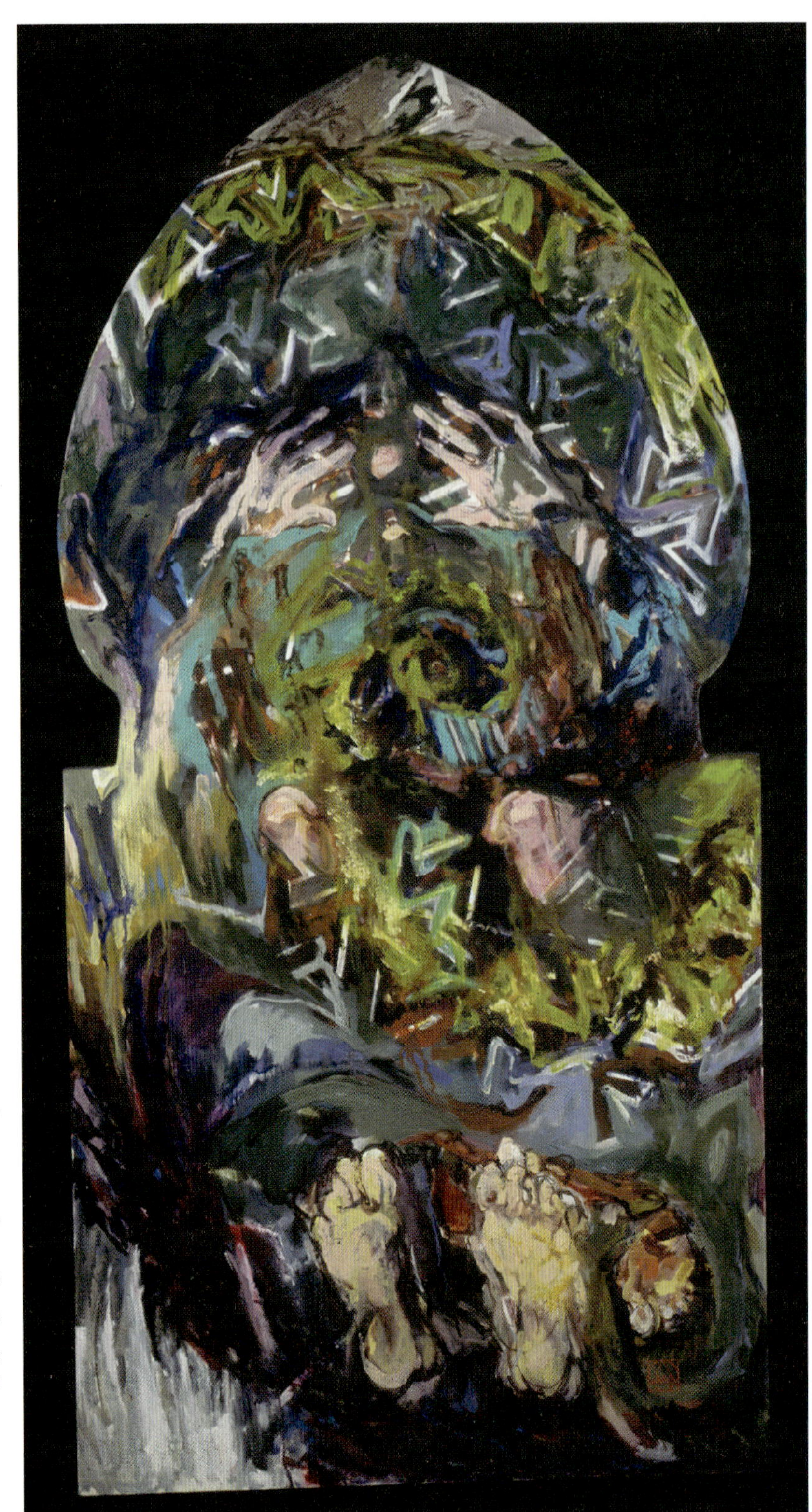

The Adoration No.3

2000
Oil/Mixed Media on Canvas
60" by 30"

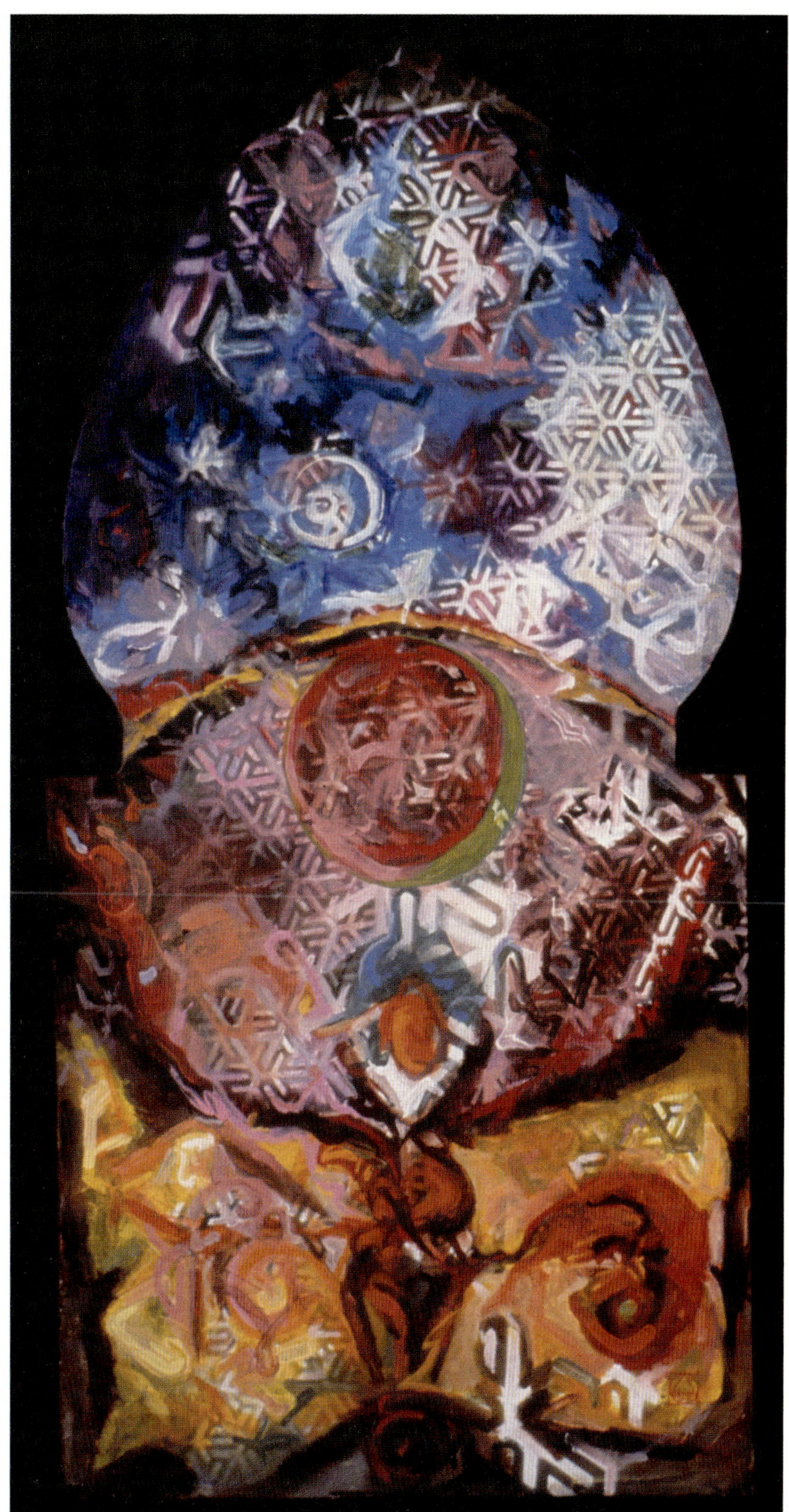

Trees of Existence: The olive neither from the east nor the west

2000
Oil on Canvas
60" by 30"

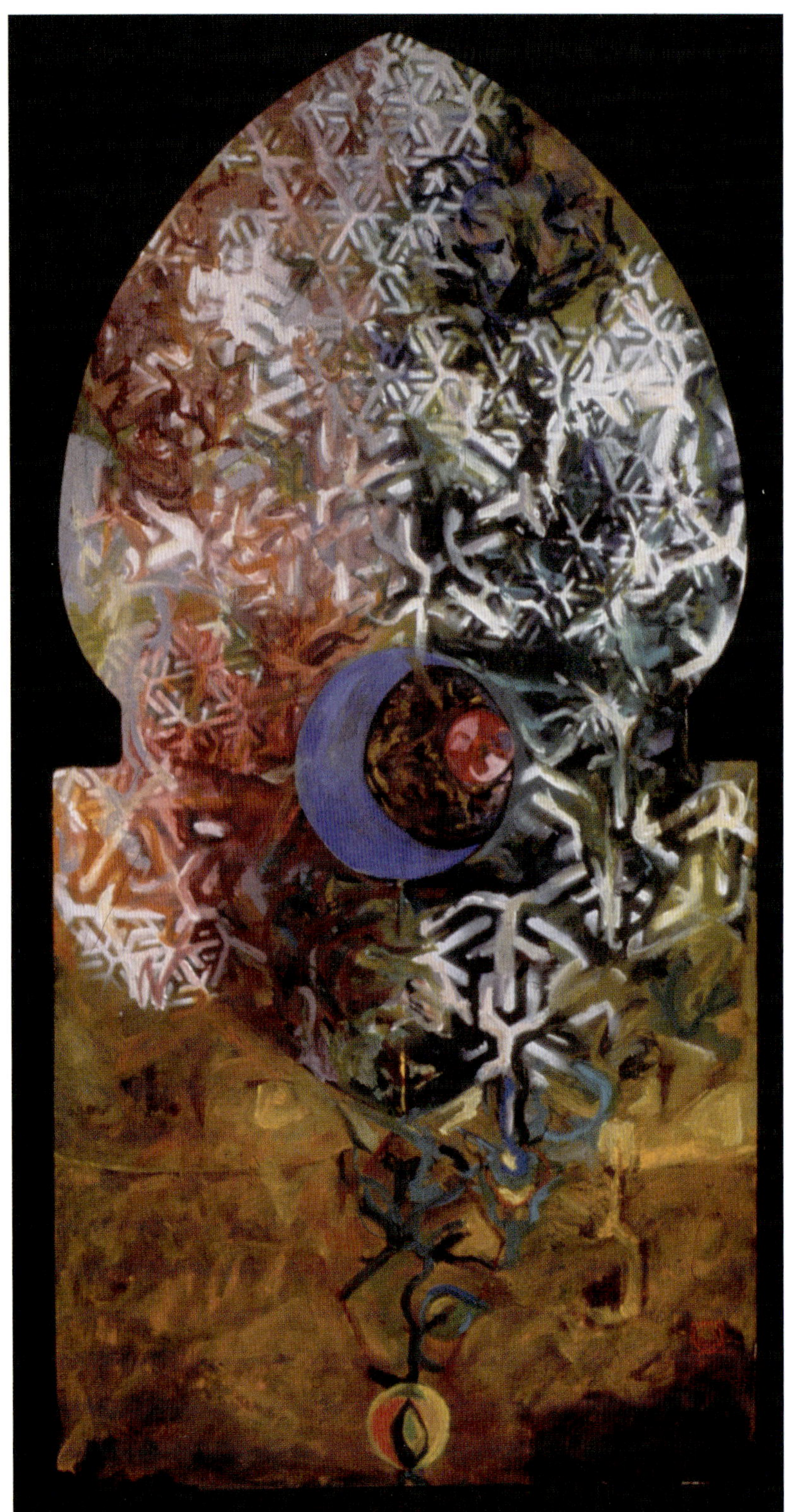

Trees of Existence: The Tree of Light

2000
Oil/Mixed Media on Canvas
60" by 30"

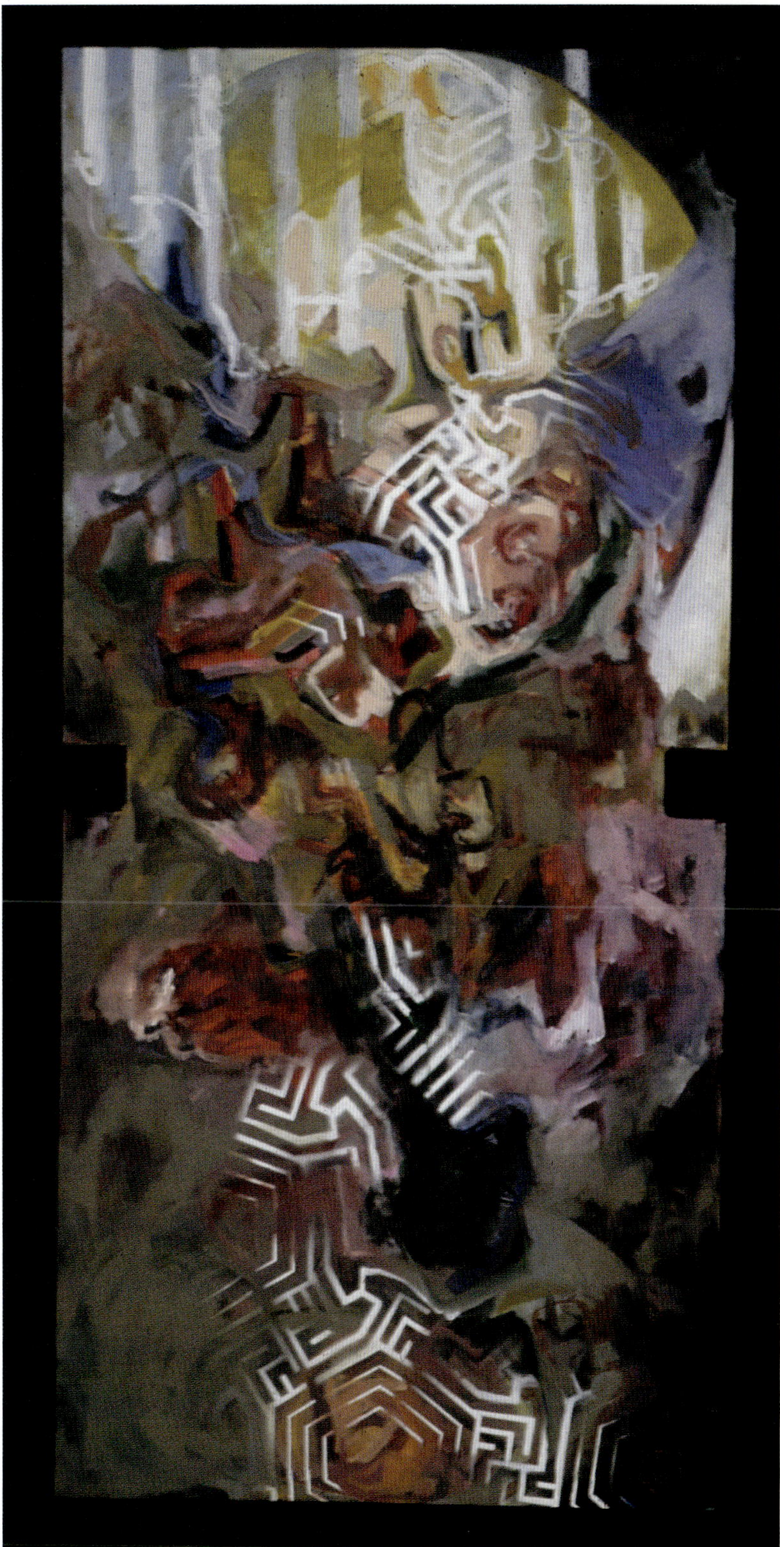

Trees of Existence: The tree of Light II

2000
Oil/Mixed Media on Canvas
60" by 30"

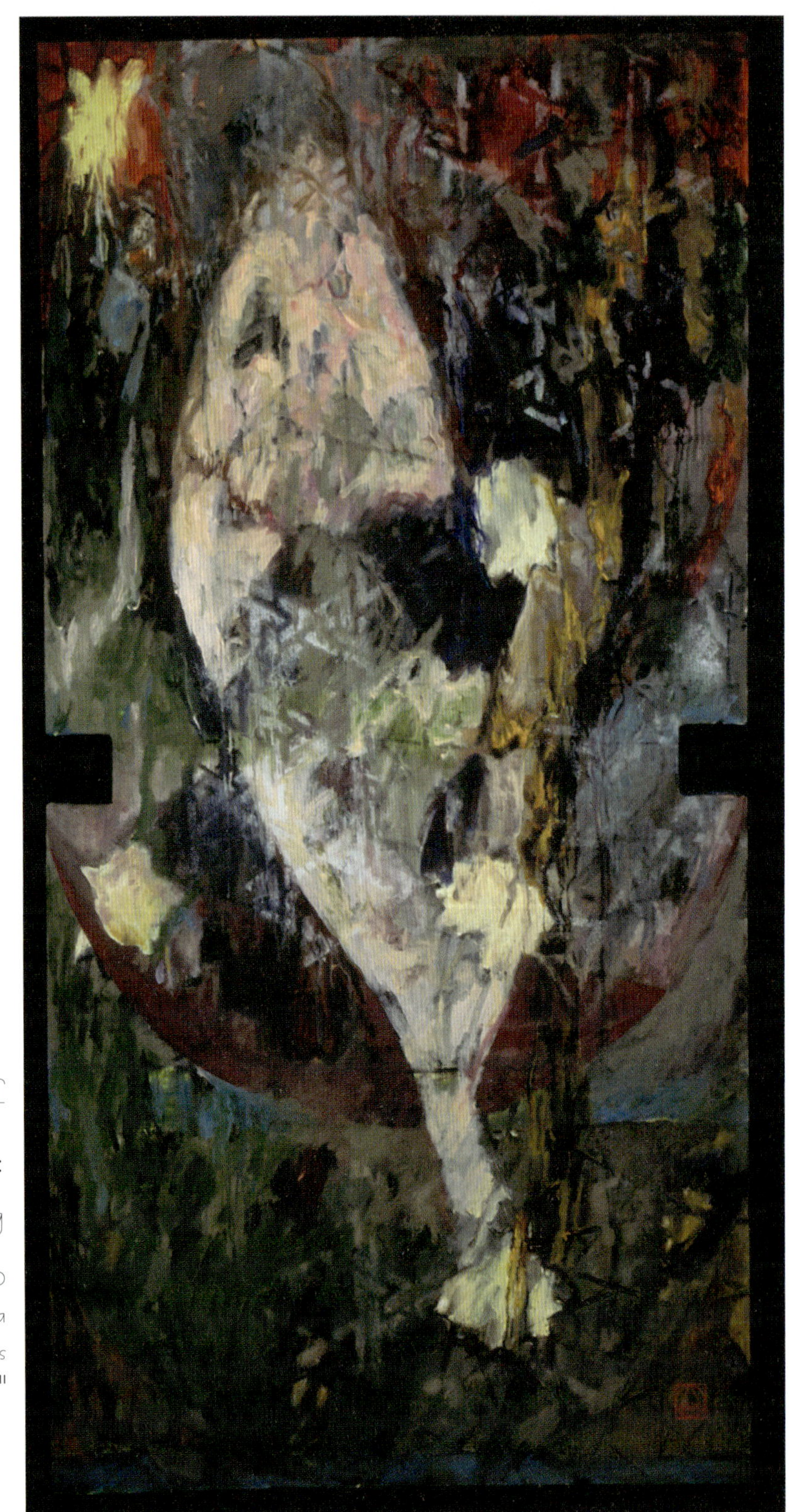

Trees of Existence: The Shining

2000
Oil/Mixed Media on Canvas
60" by 30"

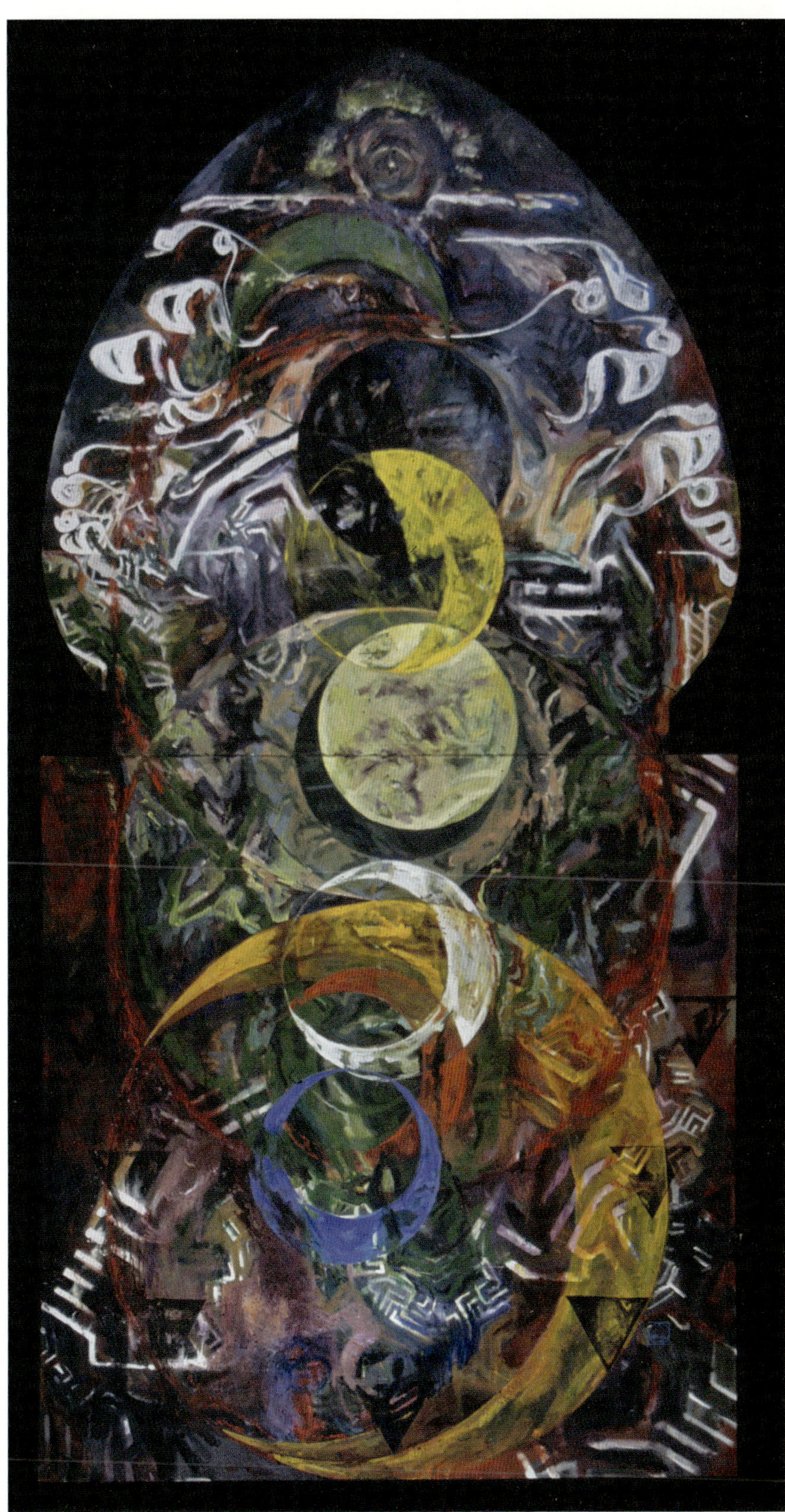

Trees of Existence: The Moon of the Seven Realms

2003
Oil/Mixed Media on Canvas
120" by 60"

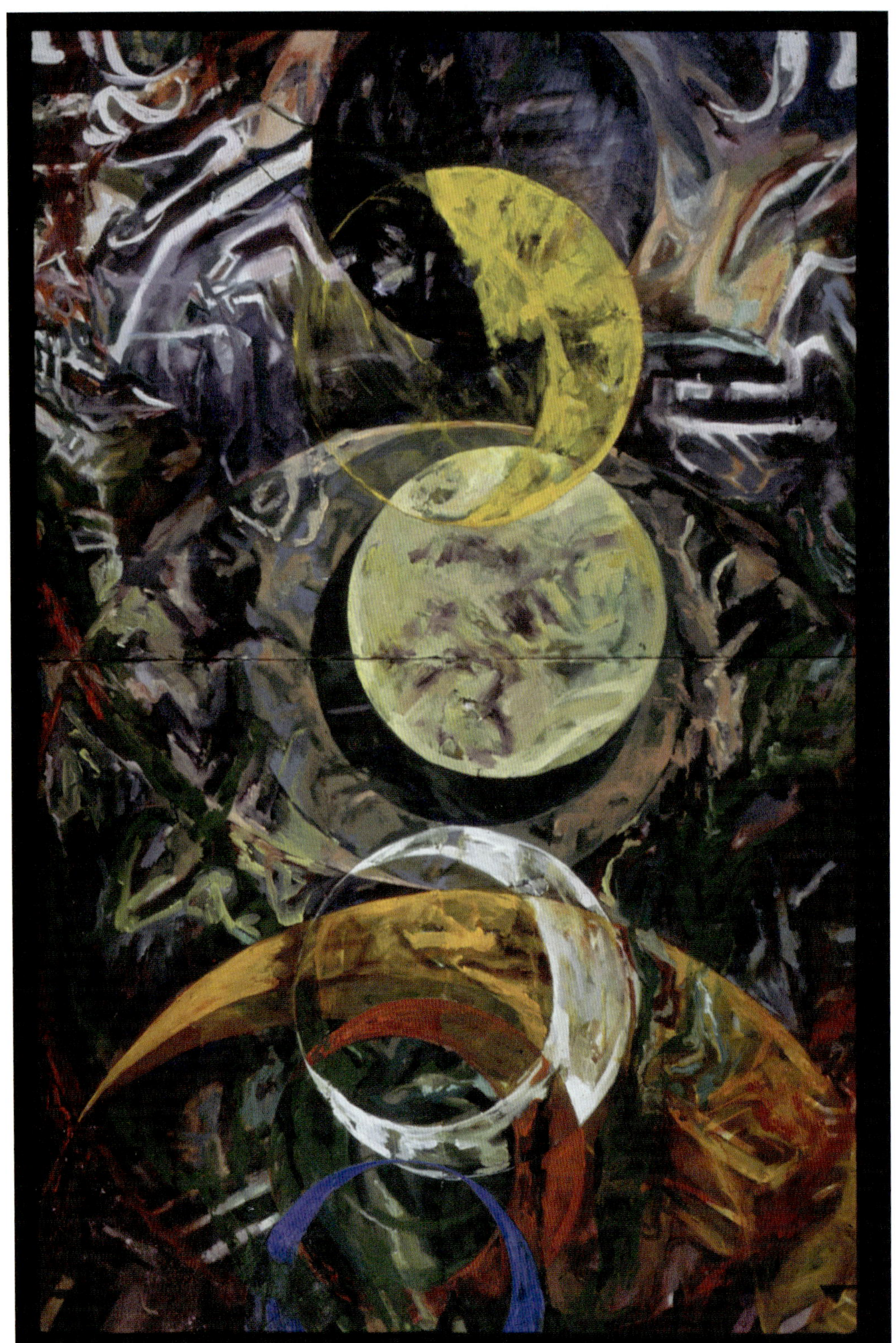

Detail of "The Moon of Seven Realms"

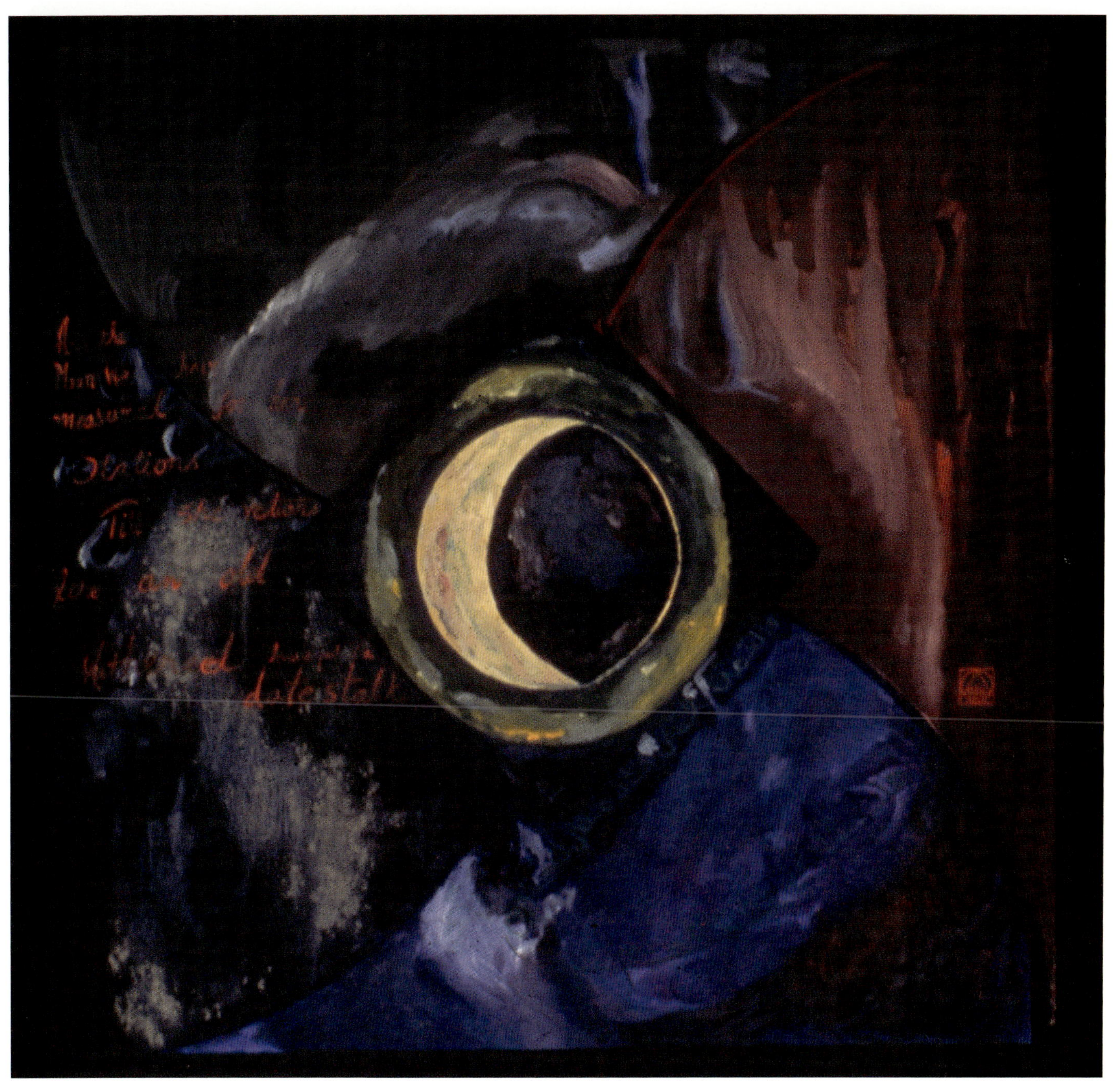

Dhikr: Remembering Father. 2003. Oil on Canvas and Wood. 40" by 40".

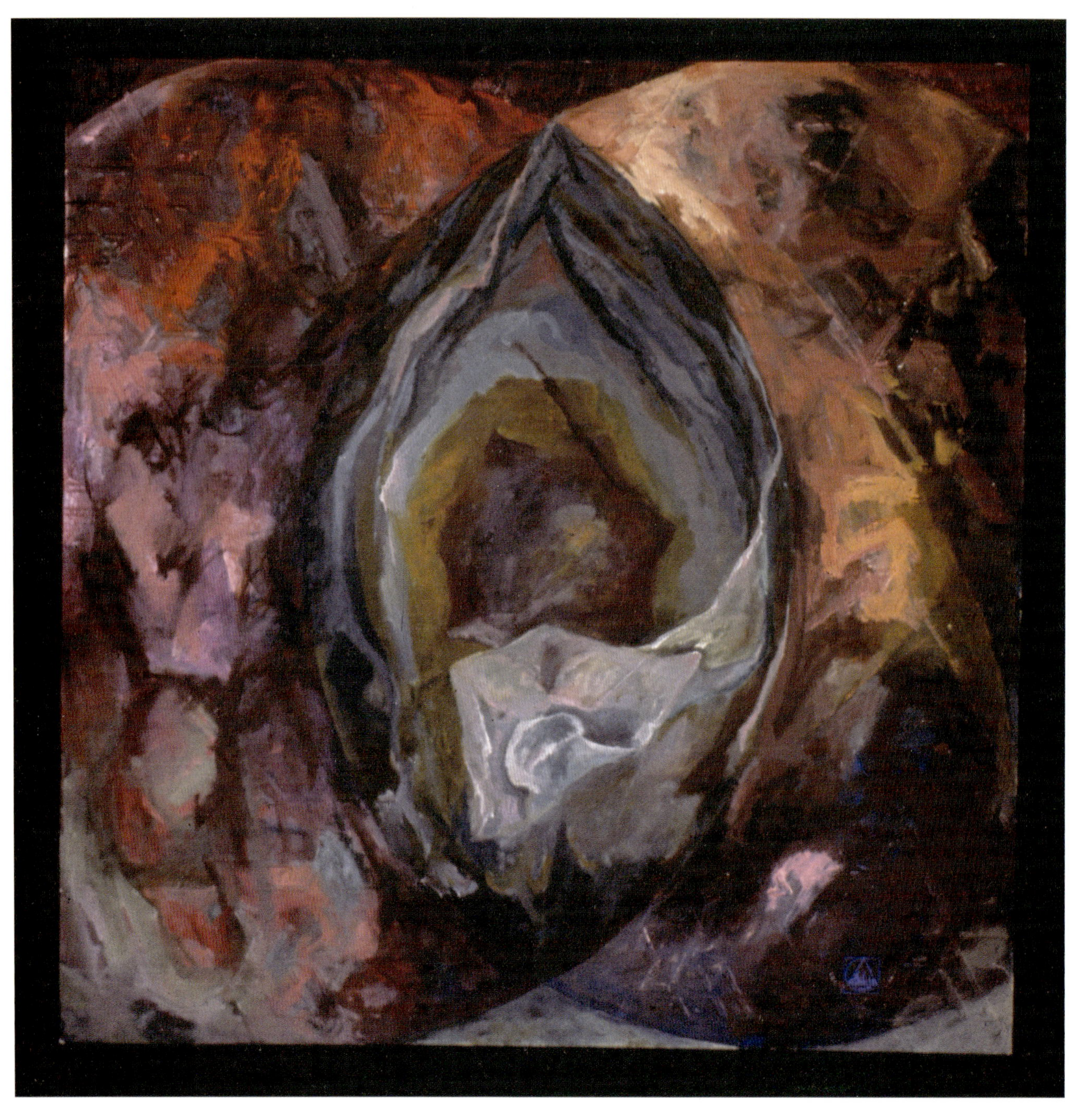

Dhikr: Remembering Adam. 2005. Oil Mixed Media on Canvas. 42" x 42"

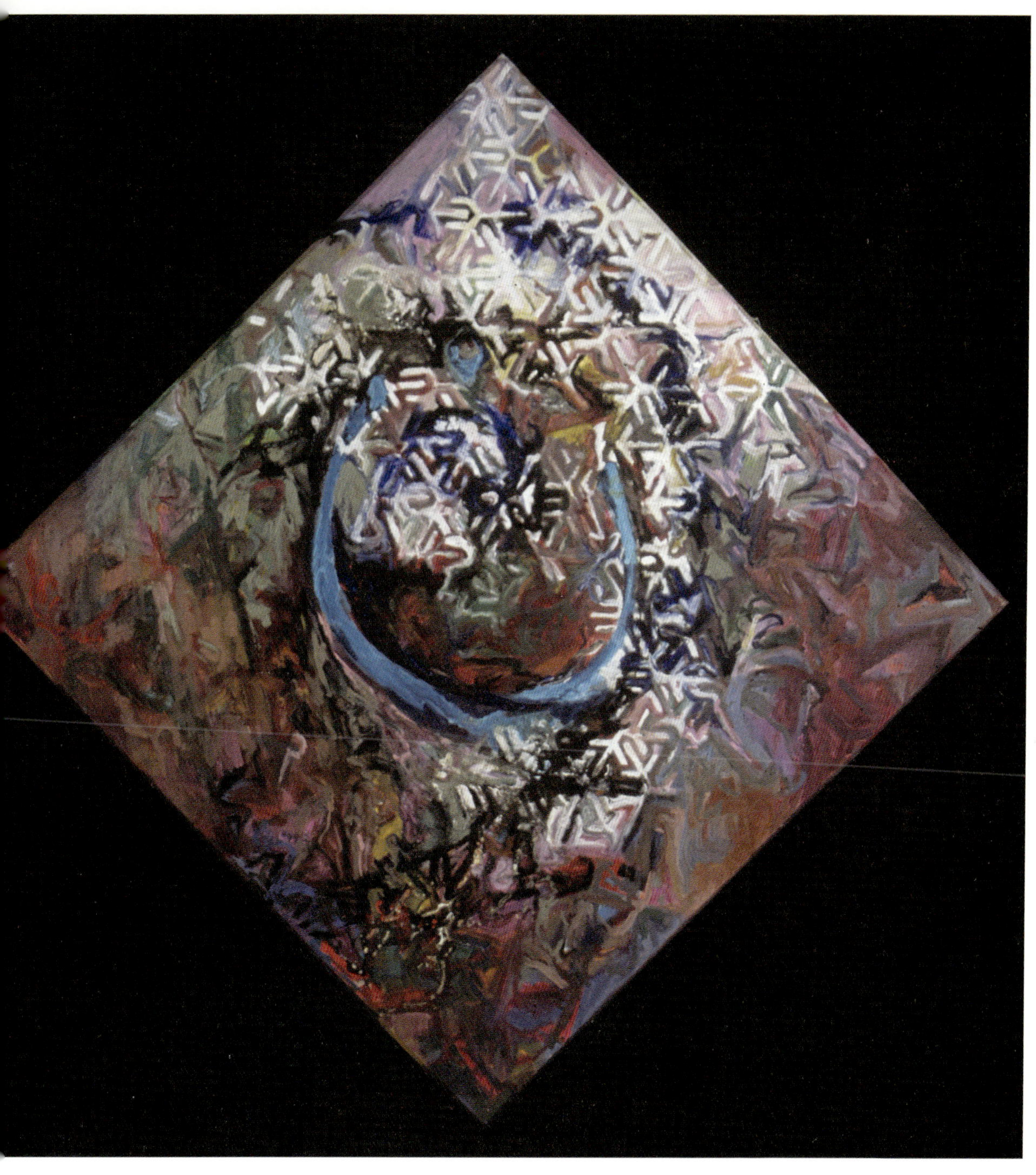

Dhikr: Remembering Noah. 2004. Oil Mixed Media on Canvas. 60" x 60"